S. Hrg. 114–449

UNDER ATTACK: FEDERAL CYBERSECURITY AND THE OPM DATA BREACH

HEARING

BEFORE THE

COMMITTEE ON HOMELAND SECURITY AND GOVERNMENTAL AFFAIRS UNITED STATES SENATE

ONE HUNDRED FOURTEENTH CONGRESS

FIRST SESSION

JUNE 25, 2015

Available via the World Wide Web: http://www.fdsys.gov/

Printed for the use of the
Committee on Homeland Security and Governmental Affairs

U.S. GOVERNMENT PUBLISHING OFFICE

20–565 PDF   WASHINGTON : 2016

For sale by the Superintendent of Documents, U.S. Government Publishing Office
Internet: bookstore.gpo.gov   Phone: toll free (866) 512–1800; DC area (202) 512–1800
Fax: (202) 512–2104   Mail: Stop IDCC, Washington, DC 20402–0001

(II)

CONTENTS

———

WITNESSES

THURSDAY, JUNE 25, 2015

ALPHABETICAL LIST OF WITNESSES

APPENDIX

UNDER ATTACK: FEDERAL CYBERSECURITY AND THE OPM DATA BREACH

THURSDAY, JUNE 25, 2015

U.S. SENATE,
COMMITTEE ON HOMELAND SECURITY
AND GOVERNMENTAL AFFAIRS,
Washington, DC.

The Committee met, pursuant to notice, at 9:31 a.m., in room SD–342, Dirksen Senate Office Building, Hon. Ron Johnson, Chair-man of the Committee, presiding.

Present: Senators Johnson, McCain, Portman, Lankford, Ayotte, Ernst, Sasse, Carper, McCaskill, Tester, Heitkamp, Booker, and Peters.

OPENING STATEMENT OF CHAIRMAN JOHNSON

Chairman JOHNSON. This hearing will come to order.

Good morning, everyone. I have been told the Director is running a little late, so we will get started without her.

Again, I would like to welcome all of our witnesses. I appreciate the time you have put into preparing your testimony. It is very informative. This is a very serious issue because earlier this month the Office of Personnel Management (OPM), announced that over the last year, hackers stole 4.1 million Federal employees' personal records. Then just days later, we learned the attack was actually far broader, involving some of the most sensitive data the Federal Government holds on its employees and likely many more records. It is hard to overstate the seriousness of this breach. It has put people's lives and our Nation at risk.

This massive theft of data may be the largest breach the Federal Government has seen to date. But it is not the first data breach affecting Federal agencies or even OPM. Unfortunately, I doubt it will be the last. Our Nation is dependent on cyber infrastructure, and that makes our future vulnerable. But cyber threats against us are going to continue to grow in size and sophistication.

The purpose of this hearing is to lay out the reality of that cyber threat and vulnerability. The first step in solving any problem is recognizing and admitting you have one. We must acknowledge we have a significant cybersecurity problem in the Federal Government, especially at OPM. This intrusion on OPM networks is only the latest of many against the agency, and OPM has become a case study in the consequences of inadequate action and neglect.

Cybersecurity on Federal agency networks has proven to be grossly inadequate. Foreign actors, cyber criminals, and hacktivists are accessing our networks with ease and impunity. While our defenses are antiquated, by comparison our adversaries are proving to be highly sophisticated. Meanwhile, agencies are concentrating their resources trying to dictate cybersecurity requirements for private companies, which in many cases are implementing cybersecurity better and cheaper.

OPM has been hacked five times in the last 3 years and has still not responded to effectively secure its network. Today's hearing will focus on the two most recent breaches.

We will hear from the OPM Inspector General (IG), Mr. Patrick McFarland, that OPM has continued to neglect information security which may have contributed to these breaches.

We will hear from Dr. Andy Ozment about the specifics of this attack as well as the Department of Homeland Security's (DHS) role in Federal cybersecurity.

Mr. Tony Scott will testify about efforts on cybersecurity across the government and the information security requirements of Federal agencies.

Finally, we will give OPM Director Katherine Archuleta an opportunity to explain how this happened on her watch, to let us know who she believes is responsible, and to clarify what we can expect from OPM going forward.

There is a bullseye on the back of USA.gov, and it does not appear this administration is devoting enough attention to this reality. We need leadership to develop and implement an effective plan to stop future cyber attacks. Without effective cybersecurity, our Nation will not be safe or secure. Cybersecurity must be a top priority.

So, again, I want to thank the witnesses and welcome everybody here to the hearing room. I am looking forward to the testimony, and with that I will turn it over to our Ranking Member, Senator Carper.

OPENING STATEMENT OF SENATOR CARPER

Senator CARPER. Thanks, Mr. Chairman. Thanks for holding this hearing, and welcome to all of our witnesses. We appreciate your being here and appreciate your service to our country.

A few weeks ago, we learned of a massive data breach at the Office of Personnel Management. Personal and financial information for more than 4 million current and former Federal employees may have been compromised. And if that is not bad enough, reports now indicate that background investigation information, some of the most sensitive personal information the Federal Government holds, may have also been compromised, potentially touching millions of additional lives.

This attack is deeply troubling and could have far-reaching consequences for a great number of people. It could have a profound impact on our national security as well.

Understandably, the public and my colleagues are upset, and they are frustrated. They want answers, and so do I, and so do this Committee. Before we leave here today, I want us to learn the answers to at least four questions:

First, what went wrong?

Second, what are we doing about it?

Third, what more needs to be done?

And, fourth, how can we help, the legislative branch, the House and the Senate?

Ultimately, sustained corrective action will be needed before we restore the public's confidence in our government's ability to keep their personal information safe and secure. I was encouraged to hear that the Office of Management and Budget (OMB) recently launched a 30-day cybersecurity sprint to further protect Federal systems from cyber attacks. That is a good start, but I think we all agree it is not enough.

As we can see from OMB's most recent annual report card on Federal network security—I think we have a table.[1] There should be a table on everybody's desk. I would just bring it to your attention.

Senator CARPER. As we can see from this table, there is a lot of room for improvement. It should be the goal of every agency, large and small, to be at the top of this table, not at the bottom.

Having said that, making it to the top of the chart does not guarantee immunity from successful cyber attacks. Too many of the bad guys are good at what they do, and they are getting better all the time. We have to bring our "A" game to the fight every single day. As we say in the Navy, this is an all-hands-on-deck moment.

For those agencies that continue to lag behind, there needs to be enlightened leadership, accountability, and a commitment to continuing improvements. One valuable cybersecurity tool that is available to all Federal agencies is the DHS program known as "EINSTEIN." I may hasten to add it is not a panacea. It is a system that can record, detect, and block cyber threats. And all of us on this Committee have recently heard about the importance of EINSTEIN after the OPM breach. The system used cyber threat information from the OPM data breach to uncover a similar intrusion which we may have never known about at the Department of Interior. That is an important discovery.

But finding out about a data breach after they occur is not good enough. We want to be able to stop these attacks before they can do any damage.

It is my understanding that the newest version of EINSTEIN—we call it "EINSTEIN 3A." I think the "A" is for "accelerated," isn't it?—can do just that. Unfortunately, today less than half of all Federal civilian agencies fall under the protection of EINSTEIN's most advanced capabilities.

Let me add again, I recognize that this system is not perfect. No one is saying that it is. No system is. But as my colleagues and our staff have heard me say many times before, if it is not perfect, let us make it better. And from everything I have heard, EINSTEIN 3A is another important and badly needed step toward that goal? That is exactly why Senator Johnson and I, along with our staff members, are working on legislation now to authorize and improve EINSTEIN with the help of some of our witnesses. This legislation will speed up its adoption across the government, require use of leading technologies, and improve accountability and oversight. I look forward to working with my colleagues on this legislation so

---

[1] The chart referenced by Senator Carper appears in the Appendix on page 90.

that we can ensure every agency is equipped with the ever improving capabilities needed to fend off cyber attacks in the future.

In closing, I think it is important to recognize the breach at OPM follows a long list of major cyber attacks against the government and, as we know, our private sector. And there are likely more to come. To tackle a challenge this big, we do need an all-hands-on-deck approach. What does this mean? Simply, it means we need all the people, resources, and authorities that we can reasonably muster to be ready to respond.

We can begin by continuing to fill the top spots in our government agencies, something on which this agency has done, personally, I think, a superb job. I am proud of the work that we have done to provide the top excellent talent to help lead the Department of Homeland Security. OPM, however, has been without a Senate-confirmed Deputy Director for nearly 4 years.

I will say that again. The Office of Personnel Management has been without a Senate-confirmed Deputy Director for nearly 4 years. It is not that the administration has not been submitting the names of qualified and talented candidates for these posts most of the time. For example, this Committee has favorably reported out the name of Navy Admiral Earl Gay, the President's nominee for this position at OPM, twice—once last year and again this year. We have done our job here on this Committee to vet him, to report him out. It is time to get him confirmed so that the Director and the agency have the help they need to right the ship.

Finally, we could also build on the cybersecurity legislation we passed last year and pass new legislation like EINSTEIN, like information sharing, like data breach. We have a job to do, and we need to do that ourselves. It would also fully fund agency security efforts.

These are all important steps we can take, but they will be incredibly difficult to accomplish if we do not work together.

Thanks, Mr. Chairman. Again, thank you all for being here. Let us have a good hearing.

Chairman JOHNSON. Thank you, Senator Carper.

It is the tradition of this Committee to swear in witnesses, so if you will all stand and raise your right hand. We will wait for the Director.

Good morning, Director. Raise your right hand. Do you swear that the testimony you will give before this Committee will be the truth, the whole truth, and nothing but the truth, so help you, God?

Ms. ARCHULETA. I do.

Mr. SCOTT. I do.

Mr. OZMENT. I do.

Mr. MCFARLAND. I do.

Chairman JOHNSON. Thank you. Please be seated.

Good morning, Director.

Ms. ARCHULETA. Good morning, and I apologize.

Chairman JOHNSON. I know traffic can be tough in Washington, DC, so I appreciate you being able to make it here.

If you are ready, we can start with you. Our first witness is OPM Director Katherine Archuleta. Ms. Archuleta is the Director of the Office of Personnel Management, a position she has held since November 2013. Prior to serving as Director of OPM, Ms. Archuleta was a senior policy adviser to then-Secretary of Energy Federico Peñ a. Director Archuleta.

TESTIMONY OF THE HONORABLE KATHERINE ARCHULETA,[1] DIRECTOR, OFFICE OF PERSONNEL MANAGEMENT

Ms. ARCHULETA. Chairman Johnson, Ranking Member Carper, and Members of the Committee, thank you for the opportunity to testify before you today. I understand and I share the concerns and frustrations of Federal employees and those affected by the intrusion into OPM's information technology (IT) systems. Although OPM has taken significant steps to meet our responsibility to secure the personal data of those we serve, it is clear that OPM needs to dramatically accelerate those efforts. I am committed to a full and compliance investigation of these incidents, and we continue to move urgently to take action to mitigate the longstanding vulnerabilities of the agency's systems.

In March 2014, we released our Strategic IT Plan to modernize and to secure OPM's aging legacy system. We began implementing the plan immediately, and in fiscal years (FY) 2014 and 2015, we directed nearly $70 million toward the implementation of new security controls to better protect our systems. OPM is also in the process of developing a new network infrastructure environment to improve the security of OPM infrastructure and IT systems. Once completed, OPM IT systems will be migrated into this new environment from the current legacy networks.

Many of the improvements have been to address critical needs, such as the security vulnerabilities in our network. These upgrades include the installation of additional firewalls; restriction of remote access without two-factor authentication; continuous monitoring of all connections to ensure that only legitimate connections have access; and deploying anti-malware software across the environment to protect and prevent the deployment or execution of cyber crime tools that could compromise our networks. These improvements led us to the discovery of the malicious activity that has occurred, and we were able to immediately share the information so that other agencies could protect their networks.

I want to share with the Committee some new steps that I am taking in addition to the steps we have already taken.

First, I will hire a new cybersecurity adviser that will report directly to me. This cybersecurity adviser will work with OPM's Chief Information Officer (CIO) to manage ongoing response to the recent incidents and complete development of OPM's plan to mitigate further incidents and assess whether long-term changes to OPM's IT architecture are needed.

Second, to ensure that the agency is leveraging private sector best practices and expertise, I am reaching out to the chief information security officers (CISO) at leading private sector companies that are experiencing their own significant cybersecurity challenges, and I will host a meeting with these experts in the coming weeks to help identify further steps.

---

[1] The prepared statement of Ms. Archuleta appears in the Appendix on page 53.

I believe that all Members of this Committee have received a copy of my action plan, and in deference to time limits, I am happy to discuss it further during the questioning.

I would like to address now the confusion regarding the number of people affected by two recent related cyber incidents at OPM.

First, it is my responsibility to provide as accurate information as I can to Congress, the public, and, most importantly, the affected individuals.

Second, because this information and its potential misuse concerns their lives, it is essential to identify the affected individuals as quickly as possible.

Third, we face challenges in analyzing the data due to the form of the records and the way they are stored. As such, I have deployed a dedicated team to undertake this time-consuming analysis and instructed them to make sure their work is accurate and completed as quickly as possible.

As much as I want to have all the answers today, I do not want to be in the position of providing you or the affected individuals with potentially inaccurate data. With these considerations in mind, I want to clarify some of the reports that have appeared in the press.

Some press accounts have suggested that the number of affected individuals has expanded from 4 million individuals to 18 million individuals. Other press accounts have asserted that 4 million individuals have been affected in the personnel file incident and 18 million individuals have been affected in the background investigation incident. Therefore, I am providing the status as we know it today and reaffirming my commitment to providing more information as soon as we know it.

First, the two kinds of data that I am addressing—personnel records and background investigations—affected different systems in two separate but related incidents.

Second, the number of individuals with data compromised from the personnel records incident is approximately 4.2 million, as we reported on June 4, and this number has not changed, and we have notified these individuals.

Third, as I have noted, we continue to analyze the background investigation as rapidly as possible to best understand what was compromised, and we are not at a point where we are able to provide a more definitive report on this issue.

That said, I want to address the figure of 18 million individuals that has been cited in the press. It is my understanding that the 18 million refers to a preliminary, unverified, and approximate number of unique Social Security numbers in the background investigations data. It is not a number that I feel comfortable at this time represents the total number of affected individuals. The Social Security number portion of the analysis is still under active review, and we do not have a more definitive number. Also, there may be an overlap between the individuals affected in the background investigation and the personnel file incident.

Additionally, we are working deliberately to determine if individuals who have not had their Social Security numbers compromised but may have other information exposed should be considered individuals affected by this incident. For these reasons, I cannot yet provide a more definitive response on the number of individuals affected by the background investigations intrusion, and it may well increase from these initial reports. My team is conducting further analysis with all speed and care, and, again, I look forward to providing an accurate and complete response.

Thank you for the opportunity, and I am happy to address any questions you may have.

Chairman JOHNSON. Thank you, Madam Director.

Our next witness is Mr. Tony Scott. Mr. Scott is the Chief Information Officer for the United States. He was appointed by the President in February of this year. His previous roles include heading VMware's global information technology group and 5 years as chief information officer at Microsoft. Mr. Scott.

TESTIMONY OF TONY SCOTT,[1] U.S. CHIEF INFORMATION OFFICER, OFFICE OF MANAGEMENT AND BUDGET

Mr. SCOTT. Thank you, Chairman Johnson, Ranking Member Carper, and Members of the Committee. Thank you for the opportunity to appear before you today. I appreciate the chance to speak with you about recent cyber incidents affecting Federal agencies.

As Federal CIO, I lead the Office of Management and Budget's Office of E-Government & Information Technology, and my office is responsible for developing and overseeing the implementation of Federal information technology policy. But today I want to focus on my team's role in facing our Nation's current reality: confronting ever-evolving cybersecurity threats.

Under the Federal Information Security Modernization Act (FISMA) of 2014—OMB is responsible for Federal information security oversight and policy issuance. OMB executes its responsibilities in close coordination with its Federal cybersecurity partners, including the Department of Homeland Security and the Department of Commerce's National Institute of Standards and Technology (NIST).

Last year, OMB announced the creation of a dedicated cybersecurity unit within my office: the E-Gov Cyber Unit. The creation of the E-Gov Cyber Unit reflects OMB's focus on conducting robust, data-driven oversight of agencies' cybersecurity programs, and the monitoring and improving of governmentwide responses to major cybersecurity incidents as well as issuing Federal guidance consistent with current and emerging technologies and risks.

This is also the team behind the annual FISMA report which highlights both successes and challenges facing Federal agencies' cyber programs. In fiscal year 2015, the E-Gov Cyber Unit is conducting oversight through CyberStat reviews and will prioritize agencies with high risk factors as determined by cybersecurity performance and incident data. Additionally, the unit is driving FISMA implementation by providing agencies with the guidance they need in this dynamic environment. One of the top fiscal year 2015 policy priorities of the team is updating something known as Circular A–130, which is the central governmentwide policy document that establishes agency guidelines on how to manage infor-

---

[1] The prepared statement of Mr. Scott appears in the Appendix on page 68.

mation resources, including best practices for how to secure those resources.

As I testified before the House last week, OMB's guidance to agencies for implementing the recently passed Federal Information Technology Acquisition Reform Act (FITARA), was issued, and it strengthens the role of the CIO in agency cybersecurity, and that is an important piece.

To further improve Federal cybersecurity infrastructure and protect systems against these evolving threats, OMB launched a 30-day cybersecurity sprint 2 weeks ago. The sprint team is comprised of staff from OMB, National Security Council (NSC), DHS, and other agencies. We have over 100 people involved in this effort, and at the end of the review, we will create and operationalize a set of action plans to further address critical cybersecurity priorities and recommend a Federal Civilian Cybersecurity Strategy.

In addition, immediately the 30-day sprint directs agencies to immediately deploy priority threat-actor indicators that have been provided by DHS to scan systems and check logs, patch critical vulnerabilities without delay, tighten policies and practices for privileged users, and accelerate the implementation of multi-factor authentication, especially for privileged users.

As I mentioned earlier, confronting cybersecurity threats is a reality I faced during my time in the private sector and continue facing in my new role as Federal Chief Information Officer. Because of this, ensuring the security of information within the Federal Government's networks and systems will remain a core focus of mine and of the administration. We are moving aggressively to implement innovative protections and respond quickly to new challenges as they arise. In addition to our efforts, we also look forward to working with Congress on actions that may further protect our Nation's critical networks and systems.

I thank the Committee for holding this hearing and for your commitment to improving Federal cybersecurity, and I would be pleased to answer any questions you may have.

Chairman JOHNSON. Thank you, Mr. Scott.

Our next witness is Dr. Andy Ozment. Dr. Ozment is the Assistant Secretary for Cybersecurity and Communications at the Department of Homeland Security where he leads several of the Department's key cyber programs. Prior to his service at DHS, Dr. Ozment was the President's Senior Director for Cybersecurity. Dr. Ozment.

TESTIMONY OF ANDY OZMENT, PH.D.,[1] ASSISTANT SECRETARY, OFFICE OF CYBERSECURITY AND COMMUNICATIONS, NATIONAL PROTECTION AND PROGRAMS DIRECTORATE, U.S. DEPARTMENT OF HOMELAND SECURITY

Mr. OZMENT. Chairman Johnson, Ranking Member Carper, Members of the Committee, I appreciate the opportunity to appear before you today. Like you, my fellow panelists, and countless Americans, I am deeply concerned about the recent compromise at OPM, and I am dedicated to ensuring that we take all necessary

---

[1] The prepared statement of Mr. Ozment appears in the Appendix on page 71.

steps to protect our Federal workforce and to drive forward the cybersecurity of the Federal Government.

As a result, I want to focus these remarks on how DHS is accelerating our efforts to protect Federal agencies and to help Federal agencies better protect themselves.

To begin with, it is important to note that we are now making up for 20 years of underinvestment in cybersecurity across the public and the private sectors. At the same time, we are facing a major challenge in protecting our most sensitive information against sophisticated, well-resourced, and persistent adversaries. This is a complex problem without a simple solution. If an easy answer were at hand, this would not be a national challenge.

To effectively address this challenge, our Federal agencies need to employ defense in-depth. Consider protecting a government facility against a physical threat. Adequate security is not only a fence, a camera, or building locks, but a combination of these measures that, in aggregate, make it difficult for an adversary to gain physical access. Cybersecurity also requires this defense in-depth, these multiple layers of security. No one measure is sufficient.

Under legislation passed by Congress last year, Federal agencies are responsible for their cybersecurity. To assist them, DHS provides a common baseline of security across the civilian government and helps agencies manage their own cyber risk through four key efforts.

First, we protect agencies by providing a common set of capabilities through the EINSTEIN and Continuous Diagnostics and Mitigation program (CDM).

Second, we measure and motivate agencies to implement best practices.

Third, we serve as a hub for information sharing.

And, fourth, we provide incident response assistance when agencies suffer an intrusion.

In my statement this morning, I will focus on the first area, how DHS provides a baseline of security through EINSTEIN and CDM. I have described the other three areas in my written Statement, and I am happy to take your questions on them.

Our first line of defense against cyber threats in the EINSTEIN system, which protects agencies at their perimeter. Returning to the analogy of a physical government facility that I mentioned earlier, EINSTEIN 1 is similar to a camera at the road onto a facility that records all traffic and identifies anomalies in the number of cars entering and leaving.

EINSTEIN 2 adds the ability to detect suspicious cars based upon a watchlist. EINSTEIN 2 does not stop the cars, but it does set off an alarm. Agencies report that EINSTEIN 1 and 2 are screening over 90 percent of all Federal civilian traffic, and they played a key role in identifying the recent compromise of OPM data hosted at the Department of Interior.

The latest phase of the program, as Senator Carper mentioned, is known as EINSTEIN 3A, and it is akin to a guard post at the highway that leads to multiple government facilities. It uses classified information to look at the cars and compare them to a watch list, and then it actively blocks prohibited cars from entering the facility. We are accelerating our efforts to protect all civilian agencies et EINSTEIN 3A. The system now protects 15 Federal civilian agencies with over 930,000 Federal personnel, or approximately 45 percent of the Federal civilian government, with at least one security countermeasure.

We have added EINSTEIN 3A protections to over 20 percent of the Federal civilian government in the past 9 months alone. During that time, and since its inception, EINSTEIN 3A has blocked nearly 550,000 attempts to access potentially malicious websites, which is often associated with potential theft of agency data.

Now, EINSTEIN 3A is currently a signature-based system. It can only block attacks or intrusions that it already knows about. That is necessary but not sufficient. We are also working on adding other technologies to the EINSTEIN 3A platform that can block never-before-seen intrusions, because EINSTEIN 3A is not just a set of existing capabilities, it is a platform upon which we can add other capabilities.

As we accelerate EINSTEIN deployment, we also recognize that security cannot be achieved through only one type of tool. That is why we need defense in-depth. EINSTEIN is not a silver bullet and will never be able to block every threat. For example, it must be complemented with tools that monitor the inside of agency networks. Our CDM program helps address this challenge.

Returning again to our analogy of a government facility, CDM Phase 1 allows agencies to continuously check the building locks inside the facility to ensure they are operating as they are intended to. Continuing the analogy, the next two phases will monitor personnel on the facility to make sure they are not engaging in unauthorized actions and will actively assess activity across the facility to detect unusual patterns of behavior.

We have purchased CDM Phase 1 capabilities for eight agencies covering over 50 percent of the Federal civilian government, and we expect to purchase these capabilities for 97 percent of the civilian government by the end of this fiscal year.

Now, the deadlines I have just told you for both CDM and EINSTEIN are when DHS provides a given capability. It takes additional time, months, for agencies to each then implement the capability for both EINSTEIN and CDM. And, of course, agencies must supplement EINSTEIN and CDM with their own tools appropriate to the needs of that existing agency.

I would like to conclude by noting that Federal agencies are a rich target, and they will continue to experience frequent attempted intrusions. As our detection methods continue to improve, we will, in fact, detect more incidents that are already occurring that we do not know about.

The recent breach at OPM is emblematic of this trend, as OPM was able to detect the intrusions by implementing best practices. We are accelerating the deployment of the tools we have, and we are bringing cutting-edge capabilities online, and we are asking our partner agencies and Congress to take action and work with us to strengthen the cybersecurity of the Federal Government.

Thank you again for the opportunity to appear before you today, and I look forward to any questions.

Chairman JOHNSON. Thank you, Dr. Ozment.

Our next and last witness is Mr. Patrick McFarland. Mr. McFarland is the Inspector General (IG) for the Office of Personnel Management, a position he has held since 1990, making him the longest-serving Inspector General in the Federal Government. He has 30 years of service in law enforcement, including 22 years at the Secret Service.

First of all, sir, thank you for your service, and we look forward to your testimony. Mr. McFarland.

TESTIMONY OF THE HONORABLE PATRICK E. MCFARLAND,[1] INSPECTOR GENERAL, OFFICE OF PERSONNEL MANAGEMENT; ACCOMPANIED BY LEWIS F. PARKER, DEPUTY ASSISTANT INSPECTOR GENERAL FOR AUDITS

Mr. MCFARLAND. Thank you. Chairman Johnson, Ranking Member Carper, and Members of the Committee, my name is Patrick McFarland. I am the Inspector General of the Office of Personnel Management. Thank you for inviting me to testify today at the hearing regarding the IT security audit work performed by our office.

I am accompanied by Lewis Parker, my Deputy Assistant Inspector General for Audits, who, with your permission, may assist in answering any technical questions you may have.

OPM has a long history of systemic failures to properly manage its IT infrastructure which may have ultimately led to the breaches we are discussing today.

First I would like to discuss some of the findings from our annual audits under the Federal Information Security Management Act. We have identified three general areas of concern, which are discussed in detail in my written testimony. They are:

One, information security governance. This is the management structure and process that form the foundation of a successful security program. It is vital to have a centralized governance structure. OPM has made improvements in this area, but we still have some concerns.

Two, security assessments and authorizations. This is a comprehensive assessment of each IT system to ensure that it meets the applicable security standards before allowing the system to operate. Our 2014 FISMA audit found that 11 of OPM's 47 systems were operating without a valid authorization.

Three, technical security controls. OPM has implemented a variety of controls to make the agency IT system more secure. However, these tools must be used properly and must cover the entire IT environment. We are concerned that they do not.

The second issue I would like to briefly discuss is the Flash Audit Alert that I issued last week. In 2014, OPM began a massive project to overhaul the agency's IT environment by building an entirely new infrastructure called "the Shell" and migrating all of its systems to that Shell from the existing infrastructure. We have two serious concerns with how the project is being implemented.

First, OPM is not following proper IT project management procedures and, therefore, does not know the true scope and cost of this project. The agency never prepared a project charter or conducted

---

[1] The prepared statement of Mr. McFarland appears in the Appendix on page 79.

a feasibility study or even identified all of the applications that will have to be moved from the existing IT infrastructure to the new Shell environment.

Further, the agency did not prepare the mandatory major IT business case, formerly known as the "Exhibit 300." This document is an important step in the planning of any large-scale IT project as it forces the agency to conduct a detailed cost-benefit analysis as well as a risk evaluation, among other things. OPM apparently believes this is simply an administrative exercise. We disagree. Because OPM has not conducted these very basic planning steps, it does not know the true cost of the project and cannot provide an accurate timeframe for completion. OPM has estimated that this project will cost $93 million; however, that amount includes only strengthening the agency's current IT security posture and the creation of a new Shell environment. It does not include the cost of migrating all of OPM's 50 major IT systems and numerous sub-systems to the Shell. This migration will be the most costly and complex phase of this project.

Even if the $93 million figure was an accurate estimate, the agency does not have a dedicated funding stream for the project. Therefore, it is entirely possible that OPM could run out of funds before completion, leaving the agency's IT environment more vulnerable than it is now.

The second major point discussed in the alert relates to the use of a sole-source contract. OPM has contracted with a single vendor to complete all of the multiple phases of this project. Unless there is a specific exception, Federal contracts are supposed to be subject to full and open competition. However, there is an exception for compelling and urgent situations.

The first phase of this project, which involves securing OPM's IT environment, was indeed such a compelling and urgent situation. That phase addressed a crisis, namely, the breaches that occurred last year. However, later phases, such as migrating the applications to the new Shell environment, are not urgent. Instead, they involve work, that is essentially a long-term capital investment. OPM has indicated that the contract for the migration phase has not been awarded. We have not been provided documentation that OPM is soliciting bids from other contractors for this work, even though this work is supposedly underway. This supports our concern that the current vendor's contract covers all phases of this project.

It may sound counterintuitive, but OPM must slow down and not continue to barrel forward with this project. The agency must take the time to get it right the first time to determine the scope of the project, calculate the costs, and make a clear plan about how to implement this massive overhaul. OPM cannot afford to have this project fail.

I fully support OPM's efforts to modernize its IT environment and the Director's long-term goals. However, if it is not done correctly, the agency will be in a worse situation than it is today, and millions of taxpayer dollars will have been wasted.

Thank you.

Chairman JOHNSON. Thank you, Mr. McFarland. I would like to start my questioning with you.

Looking back at your audits, under the Federal Information Security Management Act, if we just start with fiscal year 2009, you do not have to go much further than the first or second page of the executive summary to understand that security of the IT systems has been a problem.

In your November 5, 2009, report, you report "lack of adequate information security governance activities in accordance with legislative and regulatory requirements."

In your November 10, 2010, report, you say, "We also expanded the material weaknesses related to IT security policies to include concerns with the agency's overall information security governance and its information security management structure."

In your November 2011 report, you say, "We continue to believe that information security governance represents a material weakness in OPM's IT security program."

November 5, 2012—and this is actually pretty troubling because in the audit, the Office of Chief Information Officer (OCIO) response to your draft audit report indicated that they disagreed with the classification of the material weakness because of the progress that OPM had made with its IT security program and because there was no loss of sensitive data during the fiscal year. However, the OCIO's statement is inaccurate as there were, in fact, numerous information security incidents in fiscal year 2012 that led to the loss or unauthorized release of mission-critical or sensitive data. In other words, in the 2012 report, the Office of Chief Information Officer was in a State of denial.

November 21, 2013, second page of the report, it says, "OPM's decentralized governance structure continues to result in many instances of noncompliance with FISMA requirements; therefore, we are again reporting this issue as a material weakness for Fiscal Year 2013."

In 2014, probably the best thing you can say in terms of improvements is the material weaknesses related to information security governance has been upgraded to a significant deficiency due to the planned reorganization of OCIO. And, again, I am highly concerned about this flash audit. On the Infrastructure Improvement Project, your conclusion: "As a result, there is a high risk that this project will fail to meet the objectives of providing a secure operating environment for OPM's systems and applications." You go on to say: "In our opinion, the project management approach to this major infrastructure overhaul is entirely inadequate and introduces a very high risk of project failure."

It is pretty clear that the security of the IT system has been a problem, a material problem for quite some time. Now, when Director Archuleta came before this Committee in this Senate for confirmation, in her written answers to our questions, she said, "If confirmed as Director of OPM, improved management of OPM's IT, including proper security and data management, will be one of my top priorities. I will work with OPM's CIO and IG to ensure that adequate measures are in place to protect this vital information."

Mr. McFarland, has Director Archuleta ever met with you specifically to discuss the results of your FISMA audits?

Mr. McFARLAND. No, sir.

Chairman JOHNSON. Do you meet with her regularly?

Mr. McFarland. I meet with her at least once a month.

Chairman Johnson. To what extent have you ever discussed the material problems with the security of the IT systems of OPM?

Mr. McFarland. The memorandum in front of me is dated June 17 from us to the Director, and it spells out the Flash Audit Alert with a lot of information in it, and that was presented to her office. One week prior to that, we made sure that the chief of staff had a copy to help the flow of information for us. But we have not sat down, the Director and I, regarding this. We have not heard back other than last Tuesday when we received the response to our Flash Audit Alert.

Chairman Johnson. So do you believe that her statement that she would work with OPM's CIO and IG to ensure that adequate measures are in place to protect this vital information, do you believe she has fulfilled that commitment?

Mr. McFarland. Well, I do not believe she has fulfilled that commitment specifically with me, but I would assume—and it may be right, may be wrong—that her explanation entails the CIO's involvement with our office.

Chairman Johnson. Well, here is the problem. We have had three material breaches under her watch. In March 2014, the Chinese breached OPM looking for background investigations, and, of course, the subject of this hearing is the two most recent breaches. Director Archuleta, do you believe you have fulfilled that commitment that you made to this Committee and this Senate that you will work with OPM's IG to ensure that adequate measures are in place to protect this vital information?

Ms. Archuleta. I believe I am fulfilling that commitment, sir. With regard to the strategic plan that I promised in the confirmation, is that we have moved toward that, and your concerns about governance are exactly right. There was not a governance structure, and it was—one of the first things I did was to hire a capable and qualified CIO.

Chairman Johnson. My time is running out. Why have you not met with the Inspector General who is tasked with these audits and has given you a lot of—has basically laid out the problem for you. Why have you not met and discussed this problem with the Inspector General?

Ms. Archuleta. Thank you. We do meet on a monthly basis, and——

Chairman Johnson. But not to talk about this IT security situation.

Ms. Archuleta. The agenda——

Chairman Johnson. Which was going to be a top priority of your term.

Ms. Archuleta. Yes. The agenda is set by the IG, and he has been very helpful in identifying issues throughout the agency.

With regard to the Flash Audit, my staff and his staff are meeting on Tuesday. We have not had a meeting since his release of the Flash Audit, but he and I will followup first with staff, and then we have a meeting together. We have not, as Mr. McFarland indicated, had the opportunity to meet yet, but I am sure it was his intention and always my intention that we would sit down and discuss this, as we have with all other issues.

Chairman JOHNSON. Have you spoken to the President about this breach?

Ms. ARCHULETA. Yes, I have spoken to the President.

Chairman JOHNSON. When?

Ms. ARCHULETA. It was——

Chairman JOHNSON. About this breach, about the most recent breach of the 4.1 million to possibly 18 million records.

Ms. ARCHULETA. I did brief the President on this, and he has made it repeatedly clear that cyber threats are one of his most serious economic and national security challenges as we face the Nation, and he has in his administration pursued a comprehensive strategy, including the appointment of Tony Scott, boosting our defenses in government, and sharing more information. He has also directed the establishment of a Cyber Intelligence Center and called on the Congress to pass legislation.

Chairman JOHNSON. OK. When did you speak with the President about this?

Ms. ARCHULETA. Approximately 2 weeks ago.

Chairman JOHNSON. Do you understand the full gravity of the risk to this Nation, the risk to people's lives, government officials that are trying to protect this Nation, because of the release of this information?

Ms. ARCHULETA. Of course I do. I am as upset as you are about this. And that is why we have worked from day one to set in place the steps that had not existed there before, and I think—and if you notice in the plan that I sent you, we have taken significant steps toward that. But we are looking at nearly 30 years of a legacy system and no improvements prior to the time that I got there—not none, but not enough.

And so as you look at the improvements we have made, certainly we have made important steps, but we need to make more, and that is why we are asking Congress for their support.

Chairman JOHNSON. OK. Senator Carper.

Senator CARPER. I am going to yield my time at this point to Senator Tester, who needs to go to an Appropriations Committee markup.

OPENING STATEMENT OF SENATOR TESTER

Senator TESTER. Thank you. Thank you, Mr. Chairman. Thank you, Tom Carper. Thank you very much. I appreciate that.

Director Archuleta, was the cause of the initial breach because of the compromised credential of an employee of a contractor, KeyPoint Government Solutions?

Ms. ARCHULETA. My colleagues would be very much more able to respond to that, but, yes, the first issue was a use of credential——

Senator TESTER. A compromised credential?

Ms. ARCHULETA. A compromised credential.

Senator TESTER. You would agree with that?

Mr. OZMENT. Yes, sir, I would agree with that.

Senator TESTER. Thank you.

Director Archuleta, do you plan to continue OPM's relationship with KeyPoint?

Ms. ARCHULETA. Yes, sir. We have found that they have responded to all other remediation efforts that we have asked them to perform.

Senator TESTER. So it would be fair to say that you believe KeyPoint is able to keep its data and credentials secure at this point?

Ms. ARCHULETA. Yes, sir, I do believe that that is true. They have made important strides.

Senator TESTER. OK. IG McFarland, in your estimation has KeyPoint sufficiently updated its access to its systems to ensure that its data and credentials are secure?

Mr. McFARLAND. We do not know that at this time.

Senator TESTER. Who would know that?

Mr. McFARLAND. I would hope the CIO would know it.

Senator TESTER. OK. Has OPM updated their systems to ensure that data and credentials are secure, IG McFarland?

Mr. McFARLAND. I believe, yes, they have been working on the tactical aspect of the infrastructure, which is to update the present environment.

Senator TESTER. Do you feel that their systems are secure at this point?

Mr. McFARLAND. No, I do not feel that they are secure at this point.

Senator TESTER. OK. IG McFarland, based on what you know so far, do you believe that OPM should continue its relationship with KeyPoint?

Mr. McFARLAND. I would have to have more information. I would not be able to answer that right now.

Senator TESTER. OK. Director Archuleta, as part of your testimony, you also include recommendations to improve cybersecurity at OPM, and, clearly, in these recommendations you call on Congress for additional support in order to accelerate upgrades for OPM's IT infrastructure. Director, as a part of this additional support, are you requesting funding for additional IT software developers and IT support personnel?

Ms. ARCHULETA. We are very much focused on the additional money to improve our security. Yes, it is the primary reason for the request for additional funds.

Senator TESTER. OK. And so who have you made that request to?

Ms. ARCHULETA. We are in the process of developing that request.

We hope to have it to you by the end of this week, and we are working very closely with OMB on that.

Senator TESTER. And do you have any idea how much that will be?

Ms. ARCHULETA. I do not have the idea right now, sir, but I think there has been an initial number that we are focused in on, and I would be glad to get that to you by the end of this week.

Senator TESTER. OK. You talked about gleaning some of the information out of private sector cybersecurity. Are you going to—you said that you were going to—in your opening testimony—I do not want to put words in your mouth, but what I heard was that you were going to go to the private sector to find out some methods that they utilized?

Ms. ARCHULETA. Yes. The issue of cybersecurity——

17

Senator TESTER. And if that is correct, just say——

Ms. ARCHULETA. Yes, it is correct.

Senator TESTER. Are you going to the financial industry?

Ms. ARCHULETA. We will be going throughout the industry, and financial, I am sure, will be part of that, sir, yes.

Senator TESTER. OK, because they are getting attacked literally every night.

Ms. ARCHULETA. Yes.

Senator TESTER. And they seem to be doing a reasonable job at this point in time of fending those attacks off.

Ms. ARCHULETA. That is the type of expertise we will want to know about and learn about.

Senator TESTER. OK. Many times the private sector offers employees in software development and IT pretty damn generous benefits and pay. Yet at the Federal Government, we have had to endure Government shutdowns. In recent years, we have seen threat after threat cutting retirement, threat to cut wages, not exactly what I would say good recruiting and retention efforts.

How is OPM addressing recruiting problems, not only in your supplemental request for dollars but in general?

Ms. ARCHULETA. Thank you for that question, sir. I have actually been working very closely and had several conversations with the private sector that faces this same problem. The need for cybersecurity experts and, frankly, IT experts is one that both the public and public sector are in great need of, and we are working together with them and also working with our internal partners in all of the agencies to determine ways through hiring flexibilities, recruiting flexibilities and salary flexibilities to bring these individuals in.

What we have found is that there is a great deal of interest in public service, and this is something that we are focused in on, and the recruitment of individuals both at the Millennials and mid-career.

Senator TESTER. OK. This is for either you, Mr. Scott, or Mr. Ozment. Which one of you said that this is due to an underinvestment in cybersecurity over the last 10 years? Was that you, Mr. Ozment?

Mr. OZMENT. That was me, sir.

Senator TESTER. OK. So we are sitting here on this side of the dais. Some of us are appropriators, but we are all concerned about national security. Who should we be listening to about where we need to make those investments?

Mr. OZMENT. Ultimately you need to listen to each agency and their CIO because they know their environment best. I know that what we have come forward, the Department of Homeland Security, in our budget request for my organization, also supports governmentwide security programs, and we need a combination of those governmentwide programs and individual agencies.

Senator TESTER. Do we have a plan like that currently? Do we have a governmentwide program for cybersecurity that actually—the way I visualize it in my head, it actually has tentacles out to each agency?

Mr. OZMENT. We have a number of documents that in combination lay out our governmentwide approach, in part influenced by the recent passing of the FISMA modernization in December 2014. And so those documents in aggregate lay out the approach that we are taking.

Senator TESTER. Is that effective? I mean, is the infrastructure effective to do what we need to do? Or do we have to add to—do you understand what I am asking?

Mr. OZMENT. I do. There is always a balance between spending your time writing documents and spending your time doing the actual work.

Senator TESTER. That is true.

Mr. OZMENT. I think we are at a point right now where we have—a lot of guidance has been issued. There has been a lot of focus on how we move forward. I think we are at the point now where we need to focus on the execution.

Senator TESTER. All right. Thank you all for your testimony.

Thank you, Mr. Chairman, especially you, Mr. Vice Chairman.

Chairman JOHNSON. Chairman McCain has got to be somewhere else. We are going to let him go next, if that is OK, Senator Booker? OK. Senator McCain.

OPENING STATEMENT OF SENATOR MCCAIN

Senator MCCAIN. Thank you, Mr. Chairman. I thank Senator Booker for his indulgence.

Ms. Archuleta, the New York Times stated, "While Mr. Obama publicly named North Korea as the country that attacked Sony Pictures Entertainment last year, he and his aides have described the Chinese hackers in the government records case only to Members of Congress in classified hearings. Blaming the Chinese in public could affect cooperation on limiting the Iranian nuclear program and tensions with China's Asian neighbors."

Are you ready to state, since it has been in all public periodicals, that it was China responsible for this hacking?

Ms. ARCHULETA. I think that that would be——

Senator MCCAIN. That is a pretty simple answer. Are you ready to say that it was Chinese hacking or not?

Ms. ARCHULETA. I would have to defer to——

Senator MCCAIN. So the answer is no?

Ms. ARCHULETA [continuing]. My colleagues at State. I would defer to my colleagues at State to respond to that.

Senator MCCAIN. So the answer is no, you will not—even though it is all in public knowledge that it was China, you are not ready to tell this Committee that you know that it was China that was responsible for the hacking. Is that true?

Ms. ARCHULETA. OPM is not responsible for attribution. We rely on our colleagues to talk about that.

Senator MCCAIN. Your committee—your business is to track and to respond to hacking, and—well, I would like to go back to the issue—you said you did not know where the figure of 18 million Social Security numbers came from. This is a Wall Street Journal article. "A senior Federal Bureau of Investigations (FBI) official interjected, said it was based on her agency's own data, these people said, of 18.2 million." Are you ready to acknowledge that the FBI's number of 18.2 million is accurate?

Ms. ARCHULETA. As I stated in my opening remarks, sir, I do not believe that that is an accurate number, and I will not give an accurate——

Senator MCCAIN. So the FBI is giving us incorrect information?

Ms. ARCHULETA. I do not have an understanding of where they assumed that 18 number, but I will tell you——

Senator MCCAIN. Have you met with the FBI?

Ms. ARCHULETA. My associates have met with the FBI——

Senator MCCAIN. Your associates have, but you have not.

Ms. ARCHULETA. No, sir, I have not met with the FBI.

Senator MCCAIN. Why wouldn't you, when there is a clear situation here of an allegation by the most respected law enforcement agency in America of 18.2 million. You are alleging that it is 4 million. Wouldn't you sit down with the Director of the FBI and say, "Hey, the American people need to know, especially those 14 million between 4 and 18 million that may have been breached?"

Ms. ARCHULETA. As the head of the agency, I have many people who are working in a number of different issues. This is an important question that you have asked me, and since the time that number——

Senator MCCAIN. I guess my question, again, is: Why wouldn't you sit down with the FBI people and find out where they got their information so——

Ms. ARCHULETA. There are many——

Senator MCCAIN [continuing]. You can corroborate it or deny it?

Ms. ARCHULETA. My colleagues have met with the FBI, and——

Senator MCCAIN. But you have not.

Ms. ARCHULETA. No.

Senator MCCAIN. It does not rise to your level of attention. I see.

Now, what about the hundreds of millions of prescription drug claims and health records OPM holds to detect fraud in the Federal Employee Health Benefits Program (FEHBP)? Are those at risk?

Ms. ARCHULETA. The enrollment forms are part of the data, and as I said in my statement, again, we are analyzing the data right now.

Senator MCCAIN. You will not tell the Committee——

Ms. ARCHULETA. It does not——

Senator MCCAIN [continuing]. Whether they are at risk or not?

Ms. ARCHULETA. I will share with you that we are analyzing this data to see the scope of the impact of this breach.

Senator MCCAIN. Mr. McFarland, your office has been warning OPM about the vulnerability of its data for years. How were these warnings received by the agency, and why were they apparently ignored until it was too late?

Mr. MCFARLAND. Well, I do not know why they were ignored, but they certainly——

Senator MCCAIN. But they were ignored.

Mr. MCFARLAND. Yes, they were ignored, in my estimation.

Senator MCCAIN. So they just received it, sort of like Ms. Archuleta received the information from the FBI. It probably may not have risen to the level of her interest.

Now, Ms. Archuleta, you made an interesting statement. You told the Senate Appropriations Committee Tuesday that no one at OPM is personally to blame for the data breach. However, you told the House panel Wednesday, "I hold all of us responsible. That is our job at OPM to protect the data." In other words, everybody is responsible, so nobody is responsible. But you are responsible, and I wonder whether you think—since you said, "I hold all of us responsible," do you think you should stay in your present position?

Ms. ARCHULETA. Senator, I have been working hard from day one to correct decades of neglect, and I——

Senator McCAIN. Ignoring the——

Ms. ARCHULETA [continuing]. Continue to——

Senator McCAIN. Ignoring Mr. McFarland's warnings.

Ms. ARCHULETA. I have been here for 18 months, sir, and I have worked very hard. I think we have taken great strides not only within OPM and in partnership throughout government, cybersecurity is an enterprise effort in this administration, and I work closely with them. I am committed to continuing to do that.

Senator McCAIN. Well, unfortunately, you were not committed to heeding the warnings of Mr. McFarland, apparently, at least according to his assessment.

I guess my final question is, which I am sure you will probably obfuscate: When will the American people know, when will they know the extent of this penetration which has violated the privacy of, at least in the estimation of the FBI, 18 million people?

Ms. ARCHULETA. Thank you for that question, and as I stated earlier, we are working as rapidly as we can. I have a team that is working—that is devoted to this——

Senator McCAIN. And you have no——

Ms. ARCHULETA [continuing]. But I will be—I——

Senator McCAIN. And you have no estimate for the Committee as to when this——

Ms. ARCHULETA. When I know that the number is accurate, that is the time.

Senator McCAIN. But you cannot tell us when you would——

Ms. ARCHULETA. When I know the number is accurate.

Senator McCAIN. But you cannot tell us when.

Ms. ARCHULETA. When they bring me an accurate——

Senator McCAIN. I see.

Ms. ARCHULETA [continuing]. And I have confidence in that number.

Senator McCAIN. Ms. Archuleta, I must say that I have seen a lot of performances. Yours ranks as one of the most interesting.

I yield back.

Chairman JOHNSON. Thank you, Chairman McCain.

Because Senator Booker did yield, I will let you go before Senator Ernst.

OPENING STATEMENT OF SENATOR BOOKER

Senator BOOKER. Thank you very much. These days it is surprising to see somebody letting New Jersey go before Iowa. [Laughter.]

Senator ERNST. It is OK.

Senator BOOKER. Ms. Archuleta, I understand that the OPM Inspector General recommended the shutdown of OPM's IT infrastructure system before we knew about the hacks. Did you follow the IG's guidance? And if not, why?

Ms. ARCHULETA. I did not follow his guidance because I had to make a very conscious and deliberate decision as to the impact of the shutdown of those systems. I would have had to shut down the processing of the annuity checks to retirees. I would have had to shut down the system that does background investigations for the Federal Aviation Administration (FAA) or for the Transportation Security Administration (TSA). It would have meant that those in-dividuals and the needs that those new hires and the services they would provide would not have been able to be provided.

I made a conscious decision that we would move forward with this, but would make improvements as rapidly as possible, and we have done that. And the opportunity to work with the IG, I would say, is one that I feel is an important part of everything that we think about, but I also know that I have responsibility in many areas across OPM.

Senator BOOKER. OK. Mr. Scott, you are America's Chief Infor-mation Officer. It is obviously a very important and big task, and I want to ask you very specifically: Do you believe Ms. Archuleta and Donna Seymour are equipped to lead the efforts to shore up OPM's cybersecurity in the wake of these attacks? Do you believe that their leadership is capable of dealing with this tremendous trial?

Mr. SCOTT. I do, sir, and I have spent time on the ground with the teams that are in OPM doing the work, both from DHS and the OPM teams. They are working really hard and doing the right things. I have talked to them about the leadership that they are getting from both Director Archuleta and Donna Seymour, and they tell me that they are very supportive of the efforts and the leadership that they see there. And the one comment I would make is I think we need to be careful about distinguishing fire starters from fire fighters in this particular case, and they have my full support.

Senator BOOKER. And you have a tremendous professional back-ground. You understand the field not only in the private but the public sector. Given you know what you know going on around the country and meeting these attacks that are happening, frankly, the incredible nature of attacks going on on dozens of companies that are all name brands, things we have seen in the media, given that whole field, do you think she is the person equipped to do the job, as you say, of firefighting?

Mr. SCOTT. Yes, sir, and I have been impressed with the deploy-ment of the additional tools. I would say, the work that is going on in OPM right now would serve as a template and a model for work that other agencies need to do as well. We are learning on this across the whole Federal Government, and one of the goals of my office is to take all those lessons learned and apply them broad-ly across the Federal Government, working with my colleagues in DHS and elsewhere. We have to learn from this, and we have to be much faster as a Federal Government in responding to what is a very rising and fast rising and fast morphing set of threats. This is not a small challenge.

Senator BOOKER. I appreciate that.

Ms. Archuleta, there have been at least two instances of OPM systems being hacked. Could you just explain please how the first and second breaches occurred, what steps you have taken to prevent a future breach, and what have you done to protect the dedicated public servants who have been affected by this breach?

Ms. ARCHULETA. Certainly. Thank you for that question. The first breach occurred in April to the employee personnel records. As a result of the investigation around that, we found the second breach later. The forensic part of it I think my colleague Andy Ozment would be better able to respond to, but since that time, we have instituted even more security measures into our system, and at this time we are unaware of any other efforts to come into the system. And we are obviously monitoring that constantly 24/7 through our center.

Senator BOOKER. And if you can answer this question quickly, Dr. Ozment will have a chance to add to that question. But there have been much pointed questions toward you about the discrepancies between the numbers. The first attack, everyone was consistent. We knew what those numbers were. This attack, they are not being consistently reported, as has been pointed out by my colleagues, and we are having these varying numbers. Can you just explain why that is, hopefully leaving about 20 seconds of my 90 seconds——

Ms. ARCHULETA. Yes, that is what I mentioned in my opening statement, sir. The first incidence was 4.2 million, and we have not determined the scope of the second incident yet.

Senator BOOKER. And you had some pointed questions as to why that is, why are there varying numbers.

Ms. ARCHULETA. Because I do want them to be accurate.

Senator BOOKER. And so you are holding back giving a number until you have all the information.

Ms. ARCHULETA. We have a team that is doing the analysis even as we speak to make sure that we will announce an accurate number.

Senator BOOKER. Right, so to be premature would be to be inaccurate.

Ms. ARCHULETA. That is exactly right.

Senator BOOKER. I do have 55 seconds, sir. Could you just add a little bit more to what is being done?

Mr. OZMENT. Absolutely. I can speak to the timeline of the incident itself. In April, OPM detected this incident because they had been rolling out security capabilities over the last year and a potentially additional timeframe. So if they had not rolled out those capabilities, we would never know that this intrusion——

Senator BOOKER. So the upgrades you all were doing in order to promote better hygiene, in order to do the right things, was the reason why we detected the attack that had occurred more than a year earlier?

Mr. OZMENT. That is right. So OPM's upgrades are what detected the attack. They notified DHS, my organization, immediately. We used the information they provided to detect the second intrusion at the Department of Interior Data Center. And the team since then has been on the ground doing the forensics analysis. In May, they were able to assess with high confidence that the 4.2 million personnel records had been exfiltrated from the Department of Interior Data Center. That is OPM's data but at the Department of Interior Data Center.

In June, they assessed that some amount of information had been exfiltrated from OPM itself, but, it is complicated databases, and that is the analysis OPM is currently doing to figure out what exactly what the data that was taken.

Senator BOOKER. Thank you, Dr. Ozment.

And, Mr. Chairman, thank you for your deference to the people in New Jersey.

Chairman JOHNSON. Thank you, Senator Booker. Always looking out for the folks in New Jersey—and Iowa. Senator Ernst.

OPENING STATEMENT OF SENATOR ERNST

Senator ERNST. Thank you. Thank you, Senator Booker, and thank you, Ranking Member. Thank you, Mr. Chairman, very much.

This is a significant data breach. We will talk about this all the day, but bottom line, we need to see some action on this immediately.

Mr. McFarland, thank you for being here today. We have heard in your testimony, we have seen your Flash Audit Alert that was released by your office earlier this month, and in that audit alert, you did highlight your serious concerns regarding OPM's management of its new IT project, the improvement project. And I cannot overstate the importance of project management, particularly with respect to projects as complex and important as this particular project.

In fact, just yesterday in this Committee, we did approve a bill introduced by Senator Heitkamp and myself which will focus on improving program management in the Federal Government, and I would be interested to learn from you just a little bit more detail about your concerns to OPM's management of this IT improvement project.

Mr. McFARLAND. Yes, Senator. I think a good start here and a good example would be the fact that anyone doing a capital investment in the IT world, at least my understanding—and I can be corrected if I am wrong—by OMB's regulation is required to do a business plan known as Exhibit 300. That has not been done by OPM, yet I do hear in the last few days information that OPM and OMB are working very closely together. And I do not doubt that. But my concern is something as simple and straightforward as a business plan, if it is not completed—and we hear it is completed by OPM, and then our documentation that we requested shows that it has not been done, I would like to find out—I do not necessarily want to use this forum for my question, but I think it goes to the heart of your question. What has happened with this business plan? Has it been done or not?

Senator ERNST. And that to me is significant failure that the fact that something so simple as a business plan cannot be produced for this project, which left millions of Federal employees and their data at risk.

So, Ms. Archuleta, I do want to followup, because it sounds like now there is a request for additional dollars, and what we want to ensure is that if the dollars are allocated, that it will actually be put toward this project and that we do see results and that it is managed wisely. I cannot say that dollars we have put forth so far have been utilized maybe to the best of the taxpayers' interests.

So if you could address that, just give us that assurance that this will be handled.

Ms. ARCHULETA. Thank you. Thank you for that question. In his Flash Audit, the Inspector General recommended the completion of a major IT business case document for fiscal year 2017, and I actually look forward to discussing with the Inspector General the practical implications of completing such a document for submission for fiscal year 2017. We are in an urgent situation. I do understand, though, his concerns, and I would like to assure him that all of our decisions are being tracked, documented, and justified, and that we are working very closely with OMB.

As I mentioned earlier, I think that the Flash Audit discussions need to occur between me and the IG, and we will do that. Our staffs are meeting next Tuesday, and I am sure Mr. McFarland and I will meet immediately following. The important thing is that we address his concerns, but I think the other thing is that we move quickly. As Tony and Andy have already described, we are in a very urgent situation. So we need to balance and make sure that we are doing all the things that the IG has described, but as well, we understand the urgency of moving forward aggressively.

Senator ERNST. I do appreciate that, but this is rather late, and in retrospect we cannot go take back the data that has been captured by whoever this person or entity is out there that has gotten into the system, who has breached and gotten this data.

One thing that maybe we have not discussed yet is the fact that not only do we have millions of Federal records, and employee records that were breached, but I know when I filled out the applications for security clearances in the military, not only was my personal information on those forms, but I had to list references on those forms. Their information is also included in this.

So we have not only millions of Federal employees, potential Federal employees, but all of their reference's information is there as well. How many more millions of people are we talking about? Have we alerted those people? And what is going to be done to followup on their information as well?

Ms. ARCHULETA. Thank you for that question. It is an important question, and I agree with you totally. I am as upset as you are at the fact that these documents or this information has been breached.

Here is what we are doing, as I mentioned in my testimony, and why I cannot give a number right now. When we look at, for example, the background investigation, there is a lot of information in that. Some of that contains, if there is a—some of it does contain personally identifiable information (PII), and some of it does not. And so as we are analyzing the type of data that is in these files, those are the things that we are looking at, because we care as deeply as you do that we notify those who have been affected by this, and also understand those who have not been affected, even though you may have mentioned them in your SF–86. We are doing a complete analysis of that, and that is why I am very hesitant not to put out a number until we are absolutely sure we have looked at the whole range of possible impact.

Senator ERNST. Thank you today for the testimony.

Yes, sir?

Mr. MCFARLAND. Senator, if I may make one other point? Is it all right?

Senator ERNST. Yes.

Mr. MCFARLAND. The funding is a prime example of our concern. It is all over the board. The situation basically is in 2015 OPM is dealing with $32 million. In 2016, they are asking for another appropriation of another $21,000. In the meantime, DHS has provided them $5 million. And the other $67 million from what I understand, is supposed to come from the program areas at OPM. That is so sporadic. It just does not hold water from our perspective as to having a funding source ahead of time for the full project. It is like playing catchup, and the worst part of that is that the OPM program offices are going to be tasked to pay for that from their program office funds, appropriated funds, for the migration of each of their systems, instead of having a big picture of funding very clearly for everybody. Plus I think, the OMB is very much in favor of having transparency, and this just avoids transparency. It subsumes the money coming from program offices instead of a dedicated source of funding.

Senator ERNST. Thank you. I think that is an exceptional point.

Thank you for allowing the additional response.

Chairman JOHNSON. Thank you, Senator Ernst. I do want to point out, as best as I can determine, the information given to me, we spend something like $80 billion per year on IT systems in the Federal Government. So this is a problem of management; it is a problem of prioritization. And that is why I pointed out in my opening statement that this should be a top priority of the Federal Government. If it was made a top priority, there should be plenty of funding within the current budget to provide this kind of security. Senator Carper.

Senator CARPER. It has been raised who was behind this hack, this latest hack at OPM, this series of hacks, and someone just gave me a copy of an article that quotes FBI Director Comey, and it says: "There are two kinds of big companies in the United States. There are those that have been hacked by the Chinese and those who do not know they have been hacked by the Chinese."

It goes on to say that, "They are prolific. Their strategy seems to be we will just be everywhere all the time, and there is no way they can stop us."

It goes on to say, "Bonnie and Clyde could not do a thousand robberies in the same day in all 50 States from their pajamas halfway around the world." Those are the words of James Comey. I thought I would just share them with all of you today as we reflect on our inability to do a perfect job protecting our sensitive information within the Federal Government.

I am going to go from here to a hearing on how do we fund transportation in our country, and I think there is a corollary here, Ms. Archuleta, between your failure to be able to come in and in 18 months to turn this around. I think there is a corollary here, and I will just use transportation. I think we need to be fair, OK? I am a Navy guy, I think my colleagues know. We have a tradition in the Navy. If you are the commanding officer of the ship, your ship runs aground in the middle of the night, you were sound asleep in your wardroom, we hold the captain responsible. Some people say that is not fair, but that is our tradition in the Navy. You are the captain of the ship, and so you are held responsible, whether that is fair or not.

Having said that, I am reminded of a situation where let us say—and we are not talking about personnel management. Let us say we are talking about transportation in our country. We all know we have roads, highways, bridges, and transit systems that are decrepit, failing, and we need to do something about it. Let us say we confirmed a Secretary of Transportation 18 months ago. We do not give that Secretary of Transportation the money, which we are not doing, that is needed to be able to fix our roads, highways, bridges, and transit systems. And not only that, we do not confirm a Deputy to be part of the team, the leadership team at the Department of Transportation (DOT). It has been 4 years since we have had a Deputy, and, again, in the Navy, you have a commanding officer. You are the commanding officer. The Deputy is the executive officer, and this important agency has been without an executive officer for 4 years.

Part of that responsibility is the administration because they did not send us somebody, they did not send us a name for a long time. But they did last year. They sent us a great guy, a Navy guy, Naval Academy, commanded ships, aircraft squadrons, has all kinds of credentials, and we need to get him confirmed. This Committee has done its job. Now we have to get him confirmed so you have the help that you need.

In terms of the help that you need, this Committee I think did some pretty remarkable things last year in terms of legislation. We took the old Federal Information Security Management Act and we modernized it. That is being implemented now. We said the Department of Homeland Security does not have the kind of workforce capabilities that they need to hire and retain the sort of talent that the need to fight these cyber wars. We have addressed that. You are beginning to use those skills at DHS.

We took your ops center, the so-called National Cybersecurity and Communications Integration Center (NCCIC), and made it real.

We authorized it, said this is the real deal, and let us just not pay attention to them but let us give them the authority they need. We said let us look at our Federal information technology and our acquisition systems and see what we can do to reform them and give them the kind of oomph that they require. We have done all those things. We have done all those things. But there are some things we have not done. There are some things we have not done. I have heard enough on EINSTEIN 3 in the last week that I am convinced that that is something we ought to do. And EINSTEIN 1 and EINSTEIN 2, good start, but 3, 3A is obviously important. Andy, I thought you gave us a real good explanation. I want to ask you to come back and just explain again external, internal, the idea of the building, the locks, the vault inside, and how EINSTEIN 3 actually interfaces with—I think you called it CDM, the Continued Diagnostics and Mitigation approach, which is more like the inside protection as opposed to EINSTEIN 2, which is the outside protection. Would you just run that by us again? I thought it was a very helpful explanation.

Mr. OZMENT. Certainly. The most important concept here is the concept of defense in-depth, that there is no one tool, no one security measure that solves the security challenge. Just as in a physical building you have multiple layers of security—a fence, guards, cameras, locks on doors—you have to have the same in cybersecurity.

EINSTEIN is that perimeter system. It is the fence and the guard houses and the cameras around the perimeter of the government. It is equally important that you have security on the inside. Agencies have to do more of that internal security based upon their unique needs and missions, but Continuous Diagnostics and Mitigation is a program we have to help agencies with that, where we are buying capabilities on behalf of those agencies. They choose from a menu that suits them and roll it out. And those capabilities will come in three phases.

The first phase is the equivalent of a guard that goes around and checks that all the buildings are locked, that all the doors and windows are closed, basic security measures to make sure that they are in place.

The second phase of CDM opens the doors to the buildings and checks who is on the inside. Does that person—are they authorized to be in this building? Are they doing things that they are permitted to be doing?

And then the third phase is like a very smart security guard that goes around and just says, Hey, I see something unusual, we need to look at that, because that behavior, that thing I see inside this facility, that does not belong here.

Those are the three phases of CDM looking inside the building.

EINSTEIN, which is that perimeter, the first phase was just a camera. Here are the cars coming in and out. Record the cars. If there is an unusually large number of cars, set off an alarm.

The second phase added a watch list: Hey, this particular blue car is not supposed to enter this facility. Set off an alarm.

The third phase, which we are currently rolling out, is like a gate. It is a guard house and a gate. The gate stops the malicious car from entering the facility, but the other great thing is, because it is a guard house, we can add different security capabilities to it. We can add new cameras. We can add new gates, additional guards. It is a platform that we can add new capabilities to over time.

So while we are first focused on rolling it out across the government and building that first gate, we are also looking to the future and saying what other capabilities can we add to this guard house.

Senator CARPER. Excellent explanation. Thank you so much.

Chairman JOHNSON. Senator Lankford.

OPENING STATEMENT OF SENATOR LANKFORD

Senator LANKFORD. Thank you. Thanks for all your preparation and being here. I know this is not what you wanted to be able to do today. There are lots of other things you would like to be able to do outside on a beautiful day like that than be in here with us.

But we have a lot of things to be able to deal with in the days ahead on this.

Ms. Archuleta, let me clarify a couple things with you. You made the statement about the first intrusion, second intrusion, and the 4.2 is from the first intrusion. So just to clarify, none of the letters that have gone out have been connected to the breach dealing with the background security, so the letters that went out, all of them are related to the first breach, none of those letters related to the second.

Ms. ARCHULETA. That is correct, sir.

Senator LANKFORD. OK. You and I had an interaction just a couple of days ago, and we were talking about the development of the plan. By the way, I mentioned to you we had sent you a letter from the Subcommittee that I chair on this Committee, and your staff has been very prompt to be able to get back to us on that, and I appreciate that, to be able to get back on those details.

One of the questions I had asked about was the cybersecurity plan development. You had mentioned your CIO and the Chief Technology Officer (CTO) had led the effort to put this together, but one thing I am going to need clarification on, among several—and we will reply back to you formally on this—is the con-tractor that was the adviser, or was there an outside adviser to the CIO and CTO when they were putting the cyber plan, or did they completely put that plan together in-house?

Ms. ARCHULETA. No, our plan was developed in-house. The IT security plan was—the IT implementation plan was built in-house.

Senator LANKFORD. OK. Also in our interaction from a couple of days ago, I had asked about the statement that has been made about authorizing systems. There are 47 total systems that are out there, that there were 11 systems that were reported not authorized at that point. You said, no, 10 of those had been authorized, there is one of them that is an outside contractor that has not.

From the IG's testimony today, I noticed the statement: "In April, the CIO issued a memorandum that granted an extension of the previous authorizations for all systems whose authorization had already expired, and for those scheduled to expire through September 2016. Should this moratorium on authorizations continue, the agency will have up to 23 systems that have not been subject to a thorough security controls assessment. The justification for this action was that OPM is in the process of modernizing its IT infrastructure and once this modernization is complete, all systems would have to receive new authorizations anyway. While we support the OCIO's effort to modernize its systems, this action to extend authorizations is contrary to OMB guidance, which specifically States that an 'extended' or 'interim' authorization is not valid. Consequently, these systems are still operating without a current authorization, as they have not been subject to the complete security assessment process that the authorization memorandum is intended to represent. OMB does not require authorizations every 3 years if the agency has a mature continuing monitoring program in place. Our audit work has found that they do not."

So the question is: The authorizations that are in place, are they done by fiat basically of the agency saying we are working on this, or have they actually gone through the actual authorization process?

Ms. ARCHULETA. We have worked very closely with OMB, and they are aware of the process that we are using on these authorizations, and that understanding where we are in the process of moving toward new systems. So we have complete concurrence with OMB on these authorizations. So we are in compliance, and we are working on the final one that we noted as rapidly as possible.

Senator LANKFORD. So the question there on compliance is OMB has changed what their typical ruling is——

Ms. ARCHULETA. There are circumstances that allow us, because of the situation that we are in in terms of migrating and because of the legacy of our systems, yes.

Senator LANKFORD. OK. Mr. McFarland, any comments on that at all?

Mr. MCFARLAND. Well, that is not my understanding. My understanding is that what you just said, Senator, about the continuous monitoring exception, if it is mature. OPM does not have a mature continuous monitoring program.

Now, if OMB has made an exception, we have not been notified of that.

Senator LANKFORD. OK. The very rapid path that you had to take to deal with credit monitoring, to be able to notify and provide credit monitoring for 4 million people at this point, had to come together very quickly. My understanding of the contracting on that, you put out on a Thursday, gave 2 days and said anyone who wants to bid on this needs to have it finished by Saturday and to be able to get the bid on, and you let that out immediately the next week on that. The contractor that was involved, is that someone that OPM has used before or is familiar with? Or how did this process come together that quickly? Because that is something obviously pulling that together extremely fast.

Ms. ARCHULETA. The contracting office actually does handle that process, and on May 28, they posted the RFQ, and it closed on May 30. And they did receive several responses. We worked first with the General Services Administration (GSA) list, and we found that there were not vendors on that list that met the requirements that we needed, and that is why we moved rapidly. We wanted to be sure that we were able to notify individuals very quickly, and that is why we used a very rapid turnaround.

We also find that the companies that were—the types of services we were looking for, those companies are used to that type of timeline, and so that is why we were able to get the three responses that we did.

Senator LANKFORD. I do not know what kind of feedback you have had so far on this, and this is just one of those rolling—once things get hard, they just continue to get harder for a while. But the contractor in question that has handled this has dealt with numerous website crashes from, obviously, 4 million people hitting their site and has not been able to sustain it. Even some of my own staff that have received a letter cannot seem to get on their website and to be able to get going on the credit monitoring. So while the contractor that was placed in this was fast in the turnaround, they do not seem to be able to sustain on the other side of it. Have you had any other input on that?

Ms. ARCHULETA. I am very frustrated by sort of the initial steps that the contractor faced, and we are meeting with them on a daily basis to improve the services to our employees. Our employees deserve quick answers. They need to begin on a website. If they do not, they should not—if they cannot get to a call center employee, for example, they should not have to wait on the phone, and that is why we instituted a service similar to the Social Security Administration (SSA) where there are callbacks.

We think it has worked better, but we have learned a lot from this and are noting very carefully as we look at the next notifications, what areas we need to improve upon.

Senator LANKFORD. The questions will be—every agency head across the entire Federal family is going to want your notes from the past month, because the best thing that we can do is to be able to get our technology up to speed so that we have fewer instances like this, but also have preparation for when something actually occurs. So I hope you will be able to share some of those very quickly written notes, because there is a lot that has to be put into place to be able to help clean this up.

Ms. ARCHULETA. Thank you, sir.

Senator LANKFORD. Thank you.

Chairman JOHNSON. Senator Sasse.

OPENING STATEMENT OF SENATOR SASSE

Senator SASSE. Thank you, Mr. Chairman.

Director Archuleta, this is the fourth briefing, I believe, on this topic in the last week. It is not surprising that new details keep coming out, but I think what is frustrating and confusing for many of us is that many core elements of the timeline have shifted over the week. So I would like to just walk through a basic timeline of events and have you help me understand if we have some of these facts correct.

We heard in one setting this week that March 2014 is when OPM was first breached. That is not accurate, is it?

Ms. ARCHULETA. In March 2014, there was adversarial activity in the OPM network that dated back to November 2013, and no PII was lost during that.

Senator SASSE. How was that November 2013 breach detected and by whom?

Ms. ARCHULETA. We detected that adversarial activity, and we worked with DHS on the forensics of that.

Senator SASSE. OK. Dr. Ozment, that is your understanding as well?

Mr. OZMENT. Certainly. I will elaborate on the timeline, if you do not mind, because it is quite confusing. There was an incident in 2014, March 2014, at OPM. DHS has received a tip from an interagency partner and reached out to OPM, and we worked together and found that intrusion, as the Director noted, and that intrusion dated from November 2013.

We now, of course, have two incidents or potentially two events that are the same incident. The terminology is not great here.

Senator SASSE. That is an important distinction, though, isn't it? Because the notifications both to the Congress, potentially to folks in the White House, and ultimately to whatever the right number is, north of 10 million, all those things will be implicated based on whether or not there were one or two events.

Mr. OZMENT. There are clearly two events right now: the Department of Interior Data Center that hosted the 4.2 million OPM personnel records, and the breach at OPM itself where the analysis is still occurring to identify how much data was stolen. I think the key distinction is, who is the adversary and was it the same adversary in both cases, and for that I would have to defer to law enforcement and intelligence to speak to that. But, clearly two different locations, two different sets of data involved.

Senator SASSE. Thank you.

Director Archuleta, you said that the attackers got into OPM's network through a credential that was given to a KeyPoint contract employee who was working on background investigations, correct?

Ms. ARCHULETA. That is correct, sir.

Senator SASSE. At yesterday's hearing, we learned that no personally identifiable information was stolen in that breach, but blueprints for the main frame were. Is that your understanding?

Ms. ARCHULETA. I think we were talking about—I want to be sure which one. That was in March 2014. I think there are two different incidences that——

Senator SASSE. But what was gotten in November 2013?

Ms. ARCHULETA. In November of—OK, I am sorry, sir. I misunderstood the question. I apologize.

Senator SASSE. Thanks.

Ms. ARCHULETA. As I understand it, in November 2013, while no PII was lost, there was an extraction of some manuals. As Donna Seymour testified yesterday, as did the representative from DHS, those manuals are common manuals that could be bought in a store.

Senator SASSE. And what information was on the main frame computers that they got the manuals to?

Ms. ARCHULETA. I would have to get back with you, sir, on that. I do not know exactly.

Senator SASSE. I believe it has been reported that it was security clearance background information. Dr. Ozment, do you think that is correct?

Mr. OZMENT. I would have to defer to OPM on that.

Senator SASSE. It has been publicly reported that just a few months later, in June 2014, USIS, another OPM contractor working on security clearance investigations, reported that it had also been breached. Is that correct?

Ms. ARCHULETA. Yes.

Senator SASSE. And what was stolen from USIS?

Ms. ARCHULETA. There was OPM data impacting approximately 2.6 thousand individuals.

Senator SASSE. 2.6 thousand?

Ms. ARCHULETA. Yes.

Senator SASSE. And that was security clearance information, but it was on laptops?

Ms. ARCHULETA. I believe, sir. I would have to get back with you on that.

Senator SASSE. Earlier this week, you were asked about a separate breach at KeyPoint which was discovered in September 2014. We believe in our office that that breach occurred in August 2014 and that 49,000 security clearance holders' records were breached. Do you think that is accurate?

Ms. ARCHULETA. The adversarial activity dated back to December 2013, sir.

Senator SASSE. OK, but didn't you just a minute ago say that the only thing captured in November and December 2013 was the manuals?

Mr. OZMENT. Sir, I can jump in and speak to that.

Senator SASSE. Please.

Mr. OZMENT. The first incident that Director Archuleta is referring to is an incident that was detected in March 2014 at OPM and the activity at OPM that was detected in March 2014 dated back to November 2013.

Separately, the activity at USIS, a contractor to both OPM and DHS, dated back to April 2013. Separately, the activity at KeyPoint dated back to December 2013.

Senator SASSE. OK. So in addition to that distinction, you said in your testimony that there was an October 2014 Interior Department breach. Can you tell me what records were being housed at Interior?

Mr. OZMENT. I would defer to OPM in general, but I——

Ms. ARCHULETA. It is the employee personnel records.

Senator SASSE. So this is all non-security clearance information from the Interior breach.

Ms. ARCHULETA. The 4.2, yes.

Senator SASSE. OK. And in December 2014, what was the OPM breach in December?

Mr. OZMENT. The breach that was—that started in—my apologies.

The most recent OPM investigation where OPM is still ascertaining which background investigations were compromised was detected in April, but the activity ran from May 2014 through April, although the intruder was most active on the network from June 2014 to January 2015. I am not sure what you are referring to with the December 2014 data.

Senator SASSE. I am trying to confirm that there were security clearance background investigations in that breach as well. I think one of the reasons we care about this is because in March 2014's breach, we have been told that blueprints to the main frame were all that were stolen, and then that same main frame I believe was hacked in December 2014. And if that is true, I am wondering if any systems that did not have the manuals taken were actually hacked with secure background investigation in December 2014. If not, calling these mere "manuals" is inaccurate.

Ms. ARCHULETA. Can we get that information back to you in a full list, sir?

Senator SASSE. Sure.

Ms. ARCHULETA. So it would describe it.

Senator SASSE. We have about a 10-page letter to you on Monday, and so we would be grateful for info to that being added to that response.

Ms. ARCHULETA. We are actively responding, sir. Thank you very much.

Senator SASSE. I have more questions, but I will wait until the second round, if the Chairman wants to go first.

Chairman JOHNSON. Thank you, Senator Sasse.

Dr. Ozment, based on Senator Sasse's questions, I mean, obviously there has been a lot of activity. You combine the IG reports that have been showing the lack of security or the material problems with security. Just trying to get this all straight, it is difficult.

Is it true that DHS did write a mitigation plan based on that November 2013 attack?

Mr. OZMENT. Yes, Senator. When DHS' Incident Response Team goes onsite to any incident, as part of their report out of that incident, they say here are some of the steps that we recommend that an agency take to bolster its defenses. It is not a complete plan. It is not a, ground-up look at a network. It is based on what we saw and our time here, we recommend that you make the following changes.

Chairman JOHNSON. OK. I am not sure our Committee has access to that plan, so can you provide that to the Committee, please?

Mr. OZMENT. I will take that back, sir.

Chairman JOHNSON. I appreciate that. Rather than start a second round right away, I will just defer to Senator Portman for your first round.

OPENING STATEMENT OF SENATOR PORTMAN

Senator PORTMAN. Great. Thank you, Mr. Chairman. Thanks for having this hearing. It has been very helpful, I think, for all of us to have an exchange of information. It has also been very troubling, to be frank with you. And, one of my concerns from the start of this has been about the nature of the information that these hackers have received and specifically information that is very sensitive. As was mentioned earlier in the panel, the SF–86 is a form that you have to fill out to get a security clearance, and it includes highly confidential information, mental health history, issues about your personal life and so on that in the wrong hands can be very dam-aging, not just to that individual but also to our national security. And so one of the concerns that I would like to raise with you today is the extent to which this information you believe might be in the hands of our adversaries, and specifically, what are we going to do about that?

I realize that there are some sensitive matters here being discussed, but I think this has all been sort of out in the public, and if there is something you believe should not be discussed in this setting—I know the Chairman is very eager to get this information also—we would be happy to talk to you about it in a more classified setting.

So my first question, Dr. Ozment, is to you: Are we any closer to knowing what the scope of information was that has been accessed on this Federal Investigative Services (FIS) systems? Was it the SF–86 forms? Was it investigatory notes and supporting documents? They are also part of background information. And tell us what we know about that.

Mr. OZMENT. Senator Portman, I will start the answer to that question, and with your permission, I will ask Director Archuleta to complete it.

Anytime you are trying to assess the impact of an intrusion, you have two activities that have to take place. First, the forensic investigators have to figure out essentially where did the adversary go, what did they have access to, and what did they do with the information they had access to. And you are rarely working with full evidence. If you think about a physical crime scene, you are looking for fingerprint, you are looking—did somebody leave a half-smoked cigarette? You are looking for clues, and that is what our forensics investigators are doing. It takes time, and sophisticated adversaries try to erase their tracks. They wear gloves so they do not leave fingerprint. And that is definitely the case here.

Senator PORTMAN. So what do we know?

Mr. OZMENT. So what we know is we continue to look at systems and see where were the adversaries, were they on the system. We then have to work with OPM, and OPM has to say this is what was on the system, which means that, we can say the adversary was here. They have to be able to say this is what was on the system. And I will ask Director Archuleta to speak to that.

Ms. ARCHULETA. I am glad to speak to that. In early June, our forensics teams advised the interagency—well, they advised me, I will just say that, they advised me that there was a high confidence that the background investigation records had been compromised.

Senator PORTMAN. OK. Let me ask you another question. Dr. Ozment, there has been some discussion regarding whether these adversaries might have manipulated data in the background investigation databases that we have just heard from the Director she has high confidence that those have been breached. They could have actually manipulated data in our Federal Government systems with regard to these background investigations, for example, to change the outcome of a clearance adjudication, remove derogatory information, maybe add derogatory information.

Can you tell us anything about that possibility?

Mr. OZMENT. Sir, I can speak broadly. The adversary did have the type of access that could allow them to change information. I cannot speak to whether that change of information would allow them to do any of the things that you have specifically suggested there. I will say——

Senator PORTMAN. Is it possible?

Mr. OZMENT. It is possible to change information. The implications of that I cannot speak to. I will say—and I do not want to speak for my intelligence community colleagues, but I will repeat what they said in a prior session, which is—and law enforcement colleagues, which is they view that as unlikely.

Senator PORTMAN. Is it possible that adversaries responsible for the breaches have also manipulated the data in the background investigation data base itself?

Mr. OZMENT. I can say that the adversaries had the type of access that would allow them to manipulate some types of data. I do not know specifically what was on the databases that they had access to. I would have to defer to OPM for that.

Senator PORTMAN. Yes. Director Archuleta, one thing we talked about earlier is why we have not responded more quickly. When did you first learn about these breaches?

Mr. OZMENT. We were notified of the breach that you are describing. The first breach occurred—I will talk about both incidents. The first breach occurred in April, and——

Senator PORTMAN. April of this year?

Ms. ARCHULETA. April of this year, and we were notified of the high—as I mentioned earlier, we were notified of the second breach, the high probability of extraction or exposure in June.

Senator PORTMAN. So these background investigations we are talking about here, the highly sensitive information, we have known since June. Is that correct?

Ms. ARCHULETA. Yes, sir.

Senator PORTMAN. We did not know before that?

Mr. OZMENT. No, sir.

Senator PORTMAN. We talked earlier about your not having met with the Director of the FBI despite these incredible discrepancies in the information we are receiving from the two agencies. So I would hope the conclusion there is that you all are going to get one story for the American people. My constituents want to know, including the 10 million people who are wondering. Have you met with the Secretary of Defense or the Director of National Intelligence (DNI) about this breach in the background information database and the potential impact it could have on their employees?

Ms. ARCHULETA. I have not met with them personally, no.

Senator PORTMAN. I would think that would be another obvious thing to do. I mean, my concern, again, was the concern I think every American should share, which is the most sensitive information and the most important national security agencies has now potentially been compromised. And I would hope that the FBI Director who leads our counterintelligence efforts as well as Secretary of Defense and DNI would be involved in this effort.

Ms. ARCHULETA. May I just say that because I have not met with him does not mean that they are not engaged in this effort. The intelligence community issues are issues I know that they are meeting about, but those are not issues, as I am on the personnel records, that I am included in. But I do know that there have been meetings about that with them.

Senator PORTMAN. One final question, and this just sort of comes to me as we have been listening today to the testimony, who should have this information, the most sensitive information we talked about. The Department of Defense (DOD) used to have it. OPM has it now. Clearly, with these breaches, this should be revisited. So I would ask you, Mr. Scott, do you believe the Department of Defense is a better place to have this sensitive information? Are they better prepared to handle it?

Mr. SCOTT. I have to say, Senator, I am fairly new to the Federal Government, and I do not have a comprehensive view at this particular point. This 30-day sprint that we are doing will look across a wide range of policy, practice, organization, resourcing, and a number of other things, and that certainly we can put on our list as something to come back with——

Senator PORTMAN. The Federal Investigative Services is a specific area, Mr. Scott. We would appreciate your input as to where you think that ought to reside. I do not know if you, Mr. Ozment, or you, Ms. Archuleta, have thoughts on that.

Ms. ARCHULETA. As a suitability agent, I work very closely with our security agent and OMB to really discuss the improvements that need to be made throughout the Federal investigative background, and we have been working on that together and take very seriously that responsibility. I think we do a good job at this, and because we do work very closely with our partners on it, especially with DOD, to make sure that they are getting the type of background investigations and the quality and the timeliness that they deserve, and we are working very hard at that and making improvements all the time to be sure that we are delivering the product they deserve.

Senator PORTMAN. Thank you. My time has expired.

Chairman JOHNSON. Thank you, Senator Portman.

I just want to kind of get the timeline straight on these breaches we are talking about that are the subject of this hearing. The breach that involved personnel information occurred in December 2014 and was discovered in April of this year, about 4 months later. Is that correct, Director Archuleta?

Ms. ARCHULETA. Yes, sir.

Chairman JOHNSON. And the breach that involved all the background information, very sensitive national security background information, that occurred a year ago in June 2014, and basically took 12 months to discover. That was actually discovered because we implemented some—is it a dual authentication process and we actually prevented them from continuing to exfiltrate information?

Mr. OZMENT. Sir, if you will, I will recapitulate the full set of dates, because I think you are right, it is extremely important.

The Department of Interior Data Center—and as you know, the investigation on all of these continues, so we learn new information all the time. All of these were discovered due to the April 2015 discovery, so OPM rolled out new security technologies, as they had been rolling out new security technologies, detected an intrusion on their networks in April 2015. They gave DHS the cyber threat indicators, similar to what is being discussed in information-sharing legislation. We used those and identified the breach at the Department of Interior.

The breach at the Department of Interior, the adversary was on the network of the Department of Interior from October 2014 through April 2015. Specific pieces of data were removed in December 2014. So that is where the December date is coming out, but looking at the whole range of when the adversary was on the network, it was October 2014 through April 2015. And I would encourage you to think about as the most relevant timeframe.

Chairman JOHNSON. OK.

Mr. OZMENT. At OPM itself, there are really two key timeframes: the timeframe when the adversary was on the network, which was May 2014 to April 2015; but the time that the adversary was essentially active on the network was only June 2014 through January 2015. OPM rolled out a security control in January 2015 that stopped the adversary from taking further significant action, but it did not detect the adversary. So the adversary was largely stopped in January, but not detected until an additional control was rolled out in April.

Chairman JOHNSON. OK. Again, so we found out in mid-April, and we announced this on June 4. The public became aware of this on June 4.

Mr. OZMENT. So in mid-April, we discovered that the adversary was on the network, but not what they had done. And so we then commenced the forensics work. The forensics work reached a high confidence level more rapidly at the Department of Interior. So the Department of Interior, they more rapidly finished the forensics— or largely finished the forensics investigation and were able to conclude the breach.

Chairman JOHNSON. OK. So, again, so I understand. That takes time.

Mr. Scott, in your role within OMB as the Federal Government's Chief Information Officer, you did announce the cybersecurity sprint last week. I realize you are relatively new in the role, just starting in February, and we are not going to solve these problems overnight. I have that. Why didn't we announce a more robust effort right off the bat, basically in April?

Mr. SCOTT. So we formed an E-Gov Cyber Unit late last year in my office, put that team together, worked closely with DHS and so on. And I began with that team to look at the cross-government data. Some of the elements of what we announced in the sprint we actually started before the full sprint was announced. So it has been an escalating set of activities.

Chairman JOHNSON. So, again, you have expressed a fair amount of confidence in Director Archuleta and her team to fix this. But, again, I go back to the Federal Information Security Management Act audits, and, even in fiscal year 2009, in that audit, the first page of the executive summary says, "The lack of policies and procedures was reported as a material weakness in fiscal year 2007 and fiscal year 2008."

The weakness in our government security systems has been known for a long time. I understand that you do not solve these problems overnight. I understand that Director Archuleta has been in the office about 18 months. But certainly, having been a manager in the private sector myself—again, I do not expect perfection. I understand the problems are difficult to solve. But I am looking for people to prioritize. I am looking at people's actions that they took. And the fact that the Director did not meet with the Inspector General to specifically discuss these IG reports, the fact that she has not yet met with FBI Director Comey on these very serious issues really gives me pretty great pause in terms of having confidence that the current management team in OPM really is up to the task.

Do you disagree with that? Do you really have that great a confidence?

Again, you are the Federal Government's Chief Information Officer. Do you really have confidence in the management team of OPM that they are going to be able to solve this problem when they have shown such a lack of attention and priority to this issue? And let us face it, a record of failure now.

Mr. SCOTT. Well, Senator, I think there are several bits of evidence I can go back to, many of which you have mentioned here. But the history going back to 2009 and 2010 shows that there has been a historical set of issues there.

If I look in at OPM and elsewhere where progress has been made, I can see a delineation point from when Director Archuleta took place and recruited Donna Seymour into that role where there is a dramatic difference in terms of the actions that not only were planned, but then began execution. And I worry in this particular case that as we deploy more tools across the Federal Government and as we are likely to discover more of these kinds of issues, that there is a chilling effect on anybody wanting to come in and take one of these roles——

Chairman JOHNSON. I understand, and, again, that is a real problem. I appreciate that you are willing to exit the private sector, with your expertise and bring that to bear in terms of service to this Nation. But, again, here is my problem. A Flash Audit on the Infrastructure Improvement Project, where the final conclusion is,

"In our opinion, according to the Inspector General, the project management approach for this major infrastructure overhaul is entirely inadequate and introduces a very high risk of project failure."

That does not give me much confidence in the management team that is implementing that.

Inspector General McFarland, do you have confidence in, based on your audits, on the work you have done, do you have confidence in OPM's current management to really follow through on this and provide the security I think this Nation deserves?

Mr. MCFARLAND. I believe that the interest and the intent is there, but based on what we have found, no.

Chairman JOHNSON. I have no further questions. Senator Ayotte.

OPENING STATEMENT OF SENATOR AYOTTE

Senator AYOTTE. Thank you. I wanted to ask about—one of my staff members received a letter from OPM, and as I understand it, in the letter she was asked by a third-party contractor to produce information on her credit card and bank accounts, and she was also not told about the IRS' IP PIN program, which we have spent some time on in this Committee, which allows taxpayers who are victims of identity theft or potential victims to protect themselves.

So I was kind of troubled when I learned that this morning from her just because here we have a situation where all of these records have been breached, and if our solution is to ask people to submit additional very personal information on credit card bank records, that you would then—either you or your third-party contractor would be holding rather than working with potential victims of this to, have them seek the proper mechanism with the credit reporting agencies. So can you help me understand this and why you think this is a good approach? Because, let us face it, the fact that we are where we are with all these records that have now been breached, I do not think people should feel real confident at the moment of giving you additional information or a contractor working with the government on this.

Ms. ARCHULETA. To my knowledge, Senator, we are not asking and so I would like to talk to your—we are not asking for that information, so I would like to talk to your staff member to find out exactly what conversation or what information she got, because the registration for the credit monitoring is an action that each individual takes. So I would be glad to talk to her. I would like very much——

Senator AYOTTE. That would be great. I hope she is not already being—her information trying—identity thieves already trying to manipulate this because——

Ms. ARCHULETA. Yes.

Senator AYOTTE. When she told me that this morning, my jaw dropped. And so I want to understand why OPM is not using encryption or what steps are being taken to better use encryption of people's information given the breadth of personal information that OPM is maintaining on so many of the people in this country. Ms. ARCHULETA. Certainly. I wish that our systems, all of our systems were able to be fitted with the encryption tools, but we have an older legacy system, and there are certain applications that it would not—we would not be able to use encryption. And as Dr. Ozment will say, the encryption, in fact, would not have pre- vented this incident. That is an important fact. But that does not mean that we should not move forward to indeed apply encryption wherever we can, and we are moving forward with that as well as using more modern tools such as masking and the hiding of—or re- dacting of information when it is not needed.

Senator AYOTTE. Well, encryption is one tool in the toolbox. Does OPM employ a layered approach at all? Because, obviously, layering is something that is important when you are looking at making sure that there are different ways that information is pro- tected as a multi-verification process versus relying on one tool in the toolbox.

Ms. ARCHULETA. I would have to get back with you, Senator, to be sure that I can give you the full information.

Senator AYOTTE. Well, that would be very important, I think, be- cause to me the fact that many of the tools that seem to be lacking in the use here are already being engaged in the private sector, yet the type of personal information that is being held by an agency like OPM is just staggering in terms of what we are hearing about the breadth of this breach. So I would like a followup on that ques- tion.

One thing that I want to understand is that, in January, OPM began utilizing this two-factor authentication approach and inci- dentally, and unknowingly, ended the intrusion into the data sys- tem containing security clearance information. Do you believe that had this been in place to begin with the intrusion would not have been able to happen in the first place?

Ms. ARCHULETA. I would have to ask Dr. Ozment more on the forensics side for that, but I know that we have moved very rapidly to increase the percentage of unprivileged users with two-factor strong—two-factor authentication. We also for remote users have a 100-percent—I am sorry, that for—we have—requiring two-factor authentication for all remote users.

Senator AYOTTE. And one of the things that I had asked you about with my staff member when I told you the information she had received—and we touched upon it at the beginning—was something we heard a lot of testimony in this Committee on from the IRS Commissioner, because, unfortunately, the IRS has been breached as well, and they have this IRS IP PIN Program. It strikes me that, given the type of information that has been breached in this, the victims of this theft can very much expect that they could likely be victims of tax fraud going forward. So what steps are you taking to ensure that these victims have actual and are enrolled in the IRS IP PIN program to ensure that we are not having another hearing on I suppose potentially millions of individuals who now find themselves to be victims of tax fraud as well?

Ms. ARCHULETA. I will ask my colleague Tony Scott to talk about that. I am not familiar with the IRS.

Mr. SCOTT. Yes, the PIN program is actually designed to do a different thing, as I understand it, than would be the use case for OPM. But I can answer some of the question that you asked the Director. They do have a multilayered approach——

Senator AYOTTE. But, Tony—excuse me. I am sorry, Mr. Scott.

Mr. SCOTT. Yes.

Senator AYOTTE. But let me just say what the IRS—what I am trying to say is this, is that we know all this personal information has been breached. People are going to be—that are the victims of this will be filing their tax returns. If they are enrolled in the IRS PIN program, people cannot just file the tax return. They are then given a PIN at their physical address so, therefore, the identity thieves cannot then use this information to then victimize them on the IRS end. And this would be something, if I were a victim of this, that I would want to have put in place right away because this could protect me from potential tax fraud because of the extra step that has to be taken.

So how are we working this with the IRS to make sure these victims have access to this program? Because this is a very large problem right now.

Mr. SCOTT. Sure. I am sorry. I misunderstood your question initially. We will look at this cross-agency, not just at the IRS but anywhere else citizens need to interact with the Federal Government as part of our longer-term recommendation.

Senator AYOTTE. So, forgive me, my time is up, but I think looking at it is probably insufficient given how devastating this type of use of people's personal information can be. And I think that we cannot just look at it. I think we have to come up with a plan to give the people who have been victimized the opportunity to be part of this program so they then are not further victimized by becoming victims of tax fraud.

Thank you.

Chairman JOHNSON. Senator Sasse.

Senator SASSE. Director Archuleta, here is where I think we are. I think this morning we have heard a sketch of a timeline that shows attackers persistently coming after confidential personnel and background investigation and OPM being caught flat-footed for up to 19 months. Has any malware been detected on OPM's network since June 8 when the intrusion into security clearance data-bases was discovered?

Ms. ARCHULETA. We are unaware of any at this time.

Senator SASSE. Given how long it took OPM to detect the attacks, how can we know that the attacks are over?

Ms. ARCHULETA. We worked very closely with our cybersecurity experts throughout government, working closely not only with DHS but FBI and their hunt teams. So we are constantly monitoring our systems.

Senator SASSE. But couldn't you have given that same answer in March and it would have been wrong?

Ms. ARCHULETA. As we have developed and installed new security systems—in March 2014?

Senator SASSE. March 2015 you did not have information—you had not discovered these attacks that were then on going.

Ms. ARCHULETA. We have been working very hard, sir, to put in place all of the security measures, and I think in my plan there is a long list of things that we have done and been able to do. We need more resources to get that done, and that is why we have come to Congress to ask for them.

Senator SASSE. I want to go to Dr. Ozment in a minute, but if I can translate, I think what you just said is you do not know that the attacks are over. Director Archuleta, I am saying——

Ms. ARCHULETA. I am sorry. We——

Senator SASSE. You said you are trying hard. That is different than having knowledge that the attacks are over.

Ms. ARCHULETA. Sir, we combat over 10 million attempts in a month, and so we are working very hard. I can describe to you each of the things that we have done. That is why I gave you the paper this morning so that you would have that. We have worked very hard to do that not just at OPM but with all of our colleagues. Cybersecurity is an enterprise endeavor, and that is why we work with Tony and Andy and our colleagues at FBI and National Security Agency (NSA). We do work with them on this. We are combating a very aggressive, a very well funded, and a very focused perpetrator.

Senator SASSE. I agree that we are dealing with persistent attackers, but I think you did not say that you have certainty that the attacks are over.

Dr. Ozment, do you believe the attacks are over and that we know that with certainty?

Mr. OZMENT. I spend a lot of time with both government and private sector cybersecurity experts, and I do not think any cybersecurity expert I know would ever say that we can be certain that we have blocked all intruders who are trying to get into our networks. And I think that is the State of the world that we are living in right now. It is not a condition unique to OPM. That is a universal truth for cybersecurity.

Senator SASSE. Mr. Scott, has the malware that was found at OPM been discovered on any other agency's networks?

Mr. SCOTT. I think it is a better question for Andy, but the way it works is these indicators of compromise DHS has, and then they circulate to all the other agencies. And part of our cyber sprint, we have asked agencies to go back and take a look at those.

Senator SASSE. This is not a blame allocation question——

Mr. SCOTT. Right.

Senator SASSE [continuing]. And not meant to be hostile, but isn't your title senior to his? Help us understand what your role is if that is a question for Dr. Ozment.

Mr. SCOTT. Ours is more policy and guidance. DHS has the operational responsibility in the cyber framework.

Mr. OZMENT. And, sir, I can tell you that we have, as Mr. Scott highlighted, shared these indicators to departments and agencies. We have had at least one department think that they had an intrusion, but after further forensics, it turned out not to be the case. But we continue to, ask agencies to keep using these indicators, keep looking to see if they see activity on their networks. And, of course, if anything comes up, we work with the agency to investigate it. But we have not confirmed anything additional since— other than this Department of Interior Data Center and OPM itself.

Senator SASSE. So would that mean that any other known Federal intrusions would be visible to this Committee? Are there any other cyber attacks against the Federal Government that have not been disclosed to this Committee?

Mr. OZMENT. The FISMA 2014 legislation imposed requirements for notifying the Congress on cyber intrusions and attacks. To my knowledge, any intrusion and attack that would fall into those requirements has been notified to you. There is a constant low level of activity across the government, where sort of the noise of the Internet occurs. You have low-level criminal malware. I do not know that that is—I would not expect that that is required to be reported and is not reported. But the significant activity that is covered by FISMA 2014, to my knowledge all of that has been reported to the Congress.

Senator SASSE. Thank you. I would like to go back to Senator Portman's line of questioning about the SF–86. Director Archuleta, there have been many summaries of where we are in this attack in the media that have likened this to the Target or the Home Depot attack, which is where credit card information was stored. Obviously, we are talking about something much more serious than that. I want to quote from the SF–86 for a second.

"In addition to the questions on this form, this inquiry also is made about your adherence to security requirements, honesty and integrity, vulnerability to exploitation or coercion, falsification, misrepresentation, and any other behavior or activities or associations that tend to demonstrate a person is not reliable, trustworthy, and loyal."

As those of us who have been through top secret background investigations know, they ask lots of questions about sexual history, relationships, associations, anything that could lead an individual to be coerced or blackmailed. Can you help us understand why this information would have been stored on OPM networks to begin with?

Ms. ARCHULETA. It is part of the background investigation that we do for the clearances at very high levels for classified positions, and that is part of the determination for the adjudication information.

One of the things that is important is that—in understanding this scope of this breach is to really understand how that data was saved. So I want to be sure, again, as I go back to my opening statement, is that we are looking at all of these files to see how that data was stored and sort of the impact and scope of that breach. And that is why we are taking much more careful time to do so.

Senator SASSE. In the sexual history kinds of questioning, if people named other parties, would those have been in this information?

Ms. ARCHULETA. It really is relying on the—I actually do not know what is stored in which files. I would be glad to get that to you to give you a description. I believe that, again, it is how that information is stored and what access the breach had to that.

Senator SASSE. Dr. Ozment, do you think that narrative history would be stored?

Mr. OZMENT. I cannot speak to the contents of the databases.

Senator SASSE. I think I need to yield to Mr. Carper. I have more questions, but I will wait.

Chairman JOHNSON. Senator Carper.

Senator CARPER. Thanks. Thank you for yielding. And, again, thank you all for being here. I know you have been here for quite a while, and we are grateful for your presence and your answers to our questions.

General McFarland, I am going to ask you to come back in a minute—and maybe not right now, but in a minute I am going to ask you to come back. You shared a cautionary note with us about rushing, maybe rushing so far to address this problem, fix this problem, that we actually waste money, and you sounded a cautionary note. Why don't you just go ahead and sound that cautionary note again? What did you say right at the end of your testimony, please? Because we want to move with great dispatch, and usually that is good—maybe not always, but you gave us some advice that I thought was probably worth repeating. What did you say?

Mr. McFARLAND. I said it may sound counterintuitive, but OPM must slow down and not continue to barrel forward with this project. The agency must take the time to get it right the first time to determine the scope of the project, calculate the costs, and make a clear plan about how to implement this massive overhaul. OPM cannot afford to have the project fail.

Senator CARPER. Thank you. I mentioned earlier these four legislative steps that we took last year to bolster DHS and their ability to fend off government, writ large, cyber attacks: the passage of the Federal Information Security Modernization Act; the workforce capabilities, strengthening the workforce capabilities at the Department of Homeland Security; strengthening and making real the ops center for the Department of Homeland Security; and also the passage of the Federal Information Technology and Acquisition Reform Act (FITARA).

I think in your testimony here and in other hearings we have had, almost everybody says those were the right things to do. I am not sure we are fully implementing them as quickly as we need to, but at least I think on that front we have done our job. And we are going to do oversight to make sure that the implementation is being done in an appropriate and expeditious way.

Give us our to-do list. Give us a very brief to-do list of some things on the heels of what we have done legislatively what we need to do. What do we need to do next? And just very briefly. Director, very briefly.

Ms. ARCHULETA. Yes, and as I do that, I would like to clarify perhaps a statement that the IG made in terms of the additional resources, an answer that he responded to. We requested $21 million in the President's Fiscal Year 2016 budget, but we are currently reevaluating fiscal year 2016 IT modernization needs in light of these developments, and so we would appreciate the Senate's support. And as I said, we will get back to you with that number.

Senator CARPER. All right. Thanks.

Mr. Scott, give us one thing that ought to be at the top of our to-do list.

Mr. SCOTT. Sure. I have four very quickly.

Senator CARPER. OK.

Mr. SCOTT. The first one is pass the administration's proposal for information sharing with the private sector. It will help everybody. It will help the Nation.

Second——

Senator CARPER. I actually introduced, with a slight modification, the administration's proposal, and hopefully we can get that done. God knows we need to.

Mr. SCOTT. Thank you. The second one is do not allow exceptions to the FITARA rule. That legislates good governance and good practice and helps make the CIO fully accountable in each agency.

Senator CARPER. OK.

Mr. SCOTT. We will have recommendations coming out of our sprint, and I am sure there will be a reallocation of resource and priority as a result of those recommendations.

Senator CARPER. All right. Thanks. Dr. Ozment.

Mr. OZMENT. I would second Mr. Scott's highlighting of cybersecurity threat indicator sharing legislation. I would also really emphasize the importance of passing authorizing legislation for EINSTEIN. As you know, it played a key role in this incident, and it is an important layer in our layers of defense. And one of the impediments has been that some agencies are concerned that existing legislation impedes their ability to work with us on EINSTEIN. So your clarification of that would be greatly appreciated.

Senator CARPER. All right. Thanks.

Mr. McFarland, General, give us one more thing to put at the top of our to-do list. These are helpful ideas.

Mr. MCFARLAND. I would think that it would be very helpful if FITARA and FISMA had more teeth to it from OMB's perspective. And instead of getting lists of who is doing this or who is doing that, who is delinquent, how far are they delinquent, that there would be some accountability against people.

Senator CARPER. Good. Mr. Scott, would you respond to that, please?

Mr. SCOTT. I think those are good recommendations, Senator.

Senator CARPER. OK. Given what we all know about the OPM breach, can each of you talk about some of the lessons learned, kind of looking back, we are all better Monday morning quarterbacks, but some of the lessons learned or the best practices that we should be incorporating across the government, and why haven't we already taken these steps at some of the other agencies. Do you want to go first on that, Mr. Scott?

Mr. SCOTT. Sure, I would be happy to. Some of the early things in this also leverages my experience in the private sector. If you look at where the money has gone and where most of the effort has gone, it has been to prevent the cyber attack from occurring in the first place. Even with multilayered approaches, most of that has been on prevention, but it is very clear with these persistent adversaries that some things are going to get through. They are just nasty, and they keep coming at you. And you are always going to have at some point somebody getting through.

And so as a Nation, and especially as a Federal Government, we also have to invest in technology that will allow us to quickly detect much more rapidly than we have been when there is a breach, then contain, and then quickly remediate. And so some of our recommendations are likely to be in those areas where we have underinvested, even in a history of underinvestment in cyber more broadly.

Senator CARPER. Dr. Ozment, same question, just briefly, if you would.

Mr. OZMENT. I would just second what Mr. Scott said.

Senator CARPER. That was a short answer.

The last thing I would say is, to go back to my friend Senator Sasse, the question of is this going to be the last attack, we all know it is not. Will it be the last attack if this was from the Chinese or some other source? We know it is not. And one of the takeaways for me here today is this is an all-hands-on-deck moment; we all have a responsibility. This is a shared responsibility. You have yours, we have ours. And we need to not just point fingers at one another, but to actually figure out how to join hands and be a team in this all-hands-on-deck moment. And you have my pledge to do that, and we are going to bring our best efforts to bear, and we need for you to do that as well.

Thank you.

Chairman JOHNSON. Thank you, Senator Carper.

Before I close out the hearing by giving the witnesses one last opportunity to make a closing comment, I would like to throw it over to Senator Sasse. You said you have another quick question or two?

Senator SASSE. Yes, if I could just take 3 minutes, Mr. Chairman.

First, following upon what Senator Carper just said, Mr. Scott, did OMB give OPM permission to operate without proper cybersecurity protections?

Mr. SCOTT. I am not aware of any either giving or denying permission in that particular case. What we are doing is revising our guidelines. There was an every-3-year authorization thing earlier, and that is under review right now. And we did issue guidance that allowed for more continuous authorization versus a 3-year. But that is subject to revision.

Senator SASSE. Thank you.

Dr. Ozment, did you understand—you are now being brought in to help cleanup this matter from DHS, but did DHS understand OPM's vulnerabilities prior to them being breached?

Mr. OZMENT. One of DHS and my organization's roles is to help compile the annual FISMA report to Congress, some of which we were handed today or presented today. As part of that, we compile agencies' self-reported information on their cybersecurity, and all agencies have vulnerabilities, just as all companies have vulnerabilities.

To my knowledge, we were not aware of any specific vulnerabilities that were relevant to this incident, but we are generally aware that all agencies need to make additional progress on cybersecurity.

Senator SASSE. But given some of the specific vulnerabilities at OPM, do you believe that OPM was fully honest about its problems with DHS leading up to the breach?

Mr. OZMENT. To my knowledge, yes.

Senator SASSE. I will close with this last question. The Inspector General has criticized OPM for operating a "decentralized system" of cybersecurity because it created unique vulnerabilities. Could you explain what that means and tell us if you think any other agencies are currently operating with similarly decentralized systems? Dr. Ozment, I mean it for you, but I did not know—the Inspector General leveled the criticism, but I am curious as to whether or not you think other agencies have the same vulnerability.

Mr. OZMENT. I am sorry. Would you repeat the entire question? I apologize.

Senator SASSE. You bet. The Inspector General has criticized OPM for operating with a "decentralized system" of cybersecurity which created some unique vulnerabilities. One, I wonder if you can translate what that means. And, two, I wonder if you think any other agencies have the same decentralized system.

Mr. OZMENT. Thank you. I absolutely believe that it is very difficult for an agency to secure themselves if their CIO and CISO at the agency level are not empowered. I know that that is a concern that in part prompted, in fact, the FITARA legislation, and I think that is the crux of the matter. If they are not sufficiently empowered, if IT authority is decentralized within the agency, it is extremely difficult for that agency to secure itself.

Senator SASSE. So I think that means you think that many agencies have the same problem.

Mr. OZMENT. I think there are other agencies that need to make progress in that area, absolutely.

Senator SASSE. Thanks.

Chairman JOHNSON. Thank you, Senator Sasse.

Again, I would like to offer the witnesses one last opportunity if you have a closing thought or comment. We will start with you, Madam Director.

Ms. ARCHULETA. Thank you, Chairman. I appreciate the opportunity to be here today.

I would like to take the opportunity to clarify earlier comments to Senator McCain about the 18 million number. The 18 million refers to the preliminary approximate number of unique Social Security numbers. It comes from one of the compromised systems. However, it is incomplete, and it does not provide an accurate picture of the final number, and it is one system among several, and the number has not been cross-checked against the other relevant systems.

In closing, I would state that, again, we are reevaluating our fiscal year 2016 needs. We are not seeking a fiscal year 2015 supplemental. And, again, I appreciate the opportunity to be here with you today.

Chairman JOHNSON. Thank you. Mr. Scott.

Mr. SCOTT. Thanks for having us today. I look forward to coming back to the Committee with our recommendations at the end of the 30-day sprint period and would love to engage in a further conversation with you at that point.

Chairman JOHNSON. Thank you. Dr. Ozment.

Mr. OZMENT. Thank you. Upon reflection, I would like to add to my answer to Senator Tester about Federal cybersecurity strategy. We have the skeleton of our path forward, and we can and should move out and execute on that skeleton.

I do think there is also value in continuing to flesh out that skeleton, and, in fact, I hope that that is—the 30-day surge will help us do that.

I would also thank Senator Carper again for his remarks and reiterate the importance of information-sharing legislation and also positive authorization for the EINSTEIN program.

Chairman JOHNSON. Thank you, Doctor. Inspector General McFarland.

Mr. MCFARLAND. Yes, I would like to go back to Senator Sasse's recent comment and suggest that we work very hard to centralize the governance of information technology whenever and wherever possible.

Chairman JOHNSON. Thank you, Inspector General. Again, thank you for your service. Thank you for your independence.

Mr. MCFARLAND. Thank you.

Chairman JOHNSON. I want to thank all the witnesses for the time you have spent, for your thoughtful testimony, and your answers to our questions.

The hearing record will remain open for 15 days until July 10 at 5 p.m. for the submission of statements and questions for the record.

This hearing is adjourned.

[Whereupon, at 11:59 a.m., the Committee was adjourned.]

APPENDIX

Opening Statement of Chairman Ron Johnson
"Under Attack: Cybersecurity and the OPM Data Breach"
June 25, 2015

As prepared for delivery:

Good morning, and welcome.

Earlier this month, the Office of Personnel Management (OPM) announced that over the past year hackers stole 4.1 million federal employees' personnel records. Then, just days later, we learned the attack was actually far broader, involving some of the most sensitive data the federal government holds on its employees, and likely, many more records. It is hard to overstate the seriousness of this breach. It has put people's lives and our nation at risk.

This massive theft of data may be the largest breach the federal government has seen to date. But it's not the first data breach affecting federal agencies, or even the OPM. Unfortunately, I doubt it will be the last. Our nation is dependent on cyber infrastructure and that makes our future vulnerable. The cyber threats against us are going to continue to grow—in size and sophistication.

The purpose of this hearing is to lay out the reality of that cyber threat and vulnerability. The first step in solving any problem is recognizing and admitting you have one. We must acknowledge we have a significant cybersecurity problem in the federal government, especially at the OPM. This intrusion on the OPM's networks is only the latest of many against the agency, and the OPM has become a case study in the consequences of inadequate action and neglect.

Cybersecurity on federal agency networks has proved to be grossly inadequate. Foreign actors, cyber criminals and hacktivists are accessing our networks with ease and impunity. While our defenses are antiquated, our adversaries are by comparison proving to be highly sophisticated. Meanwhile, agencies are concentrating their resources trying to dictate cybersecurity requirements for private companies, which in many cases are implementing cybersecurity better and more cheaply.

The OPM has been hacked five times in the past three years, and it still has not responded to effectively secure its network. Today's hearing will focus on the two most recent breaches.

We will hear from the OPM Inspector General, Mr. Patrick McFarland, that the OPM has continued to neglect information security, which may have contributed to these breaches. We will hear from Dr. Andy Ozment about the specifics of this attack, as well as the Department of Homeland Security's role in federal cybersecurity. Mr. Tony Scott will testify about efforts on cybersecurity across the government and about the information security requirements of federal agencies. Finally, we will give OPM Director Katherine Archuleta an opportunity to explain how this happened on her watch, to let us know who she believes is responsible, and to clarify what we can expect from the OPM going forward.

There's a bullseye on the back of USA.gov, and it does not appear this administration is devoting enough attention to this reality. We need leadership to develop and implement an effective plan to stop future cyberattacks. Without effective cybersecurity, our nation will not be safe and secure. Cybersecurity must be a top priority.

Thank you. I look forward to your testimony.

###

Statement of Ranking Member Thomas R. Carper
"Under Attack: Federal Cybersecurity and the OPM Data Breach"
June 25, 2015

As prepared for delivery:

Thank you, Mr. Chairman, for calling this very timely hearing. And welcome to all of our witnesses.

A few weeks ago, we learned of a massive data breach at the Office of Personnel Management (OPM). Personal and financial information for more than four million current and former federal employees may have been compromised. As if that was not bad enough, reports now indicate that background investigation information - some of the most sensitive personal information the federal government holds – may also have been compromised, potentially touching millions of additional individuals.

This attack is deeply troubling and could have far-reaching consequences for a great number of people. It could have a profound impact on our national security, as well.

Understandably, the public and my colleagues are upset, and they are frustrated. They want answers. So do I, and so does this Committee. Before we leave here today, I want us to learn the answers to at least four questions: First, what went wrong? Second, what are we doing about it? Third, what more needs to be done? And, fourth, how can Congress help?

Ultimately, sustained corrective action will be needed before we restore the public's confidence in our government's ability to keep their personal information safe and secure.

I was encouraged to hear that OMB recently launched a 30-day "cybersecurity sprint" to further protect federal systems from cyber attacks. This is a good start, but I think we can all agree it's not enough.

As we can see from OMB's most recent annual report card on federal network security, there is much room for improvement. It should be the goal of every agency – large and small – to be at the top of this table. Having said that, making it to the top of this chart does not guarantee immunity from a successful cyber attack. Too many of the bad guys are good at what they do, and they're getting better all the time. We've got to bring our 'A' game to this fight every day. It's all hands on deck all the time.

For those agencies that continue to lag behind, there needs to be enlightened leadership, accountability and a commitment to continuing improvements.

One valuable cybersecurity tool that is available to all federal agencies is a Department of Homeland Security (DHS) program known as EINSTEIN. It is not a panacea. It is a system that can record, detect, and block cyber threats.

All of us on this committee have recently heard about the importance of EINSTEIN after the OPM breach. This system used cyber threat information from the OPM data breach to uncover a similar intrusion – which we may have never known about – at the Department of Interior. That was an important discovery. But finding out about data breaches after they occur isn't good enough. We want to be able to stop these attacks before they can do any damage.

It is my understanding that the newest version of EINSTEIN – EINSTEIN 3A – can do just that. Unfortunately, today, less than half of all federal civilian agencies fall under the protection of EINSTEIN's most advanced capabilities.

I recognize this system is not perfect – no system is. But, as my colleagues and our staffs have heard me say many times, if it isn't perfect, make it better. From everything I've heard, EINSTEIN 3A is another important and badly needed step toward that goal.

And that is exactly why Senator Johnson and I – along with our staff members – are working on legislation now to authorize and improve EINSTEIN. This legislation would speed up its adoption across the government, require use of leading technologies, and improve accountability and oversight.

I look forward to working with my colleagues on this legislation so that we can ensure every agency is equipped with the ever-improving capabilities needed to fend off cyber attacks in the future. In closing, I think it's important to recognize the breach at OPM follows a long list of major cyber attacks against the government, as well as the private sector. And, there is likely more to come.

To tackle a challenge this big, we need an 'all hands on deck' approach. What does this mean? Simple, we need all the people, resources, and authorities we can reasonably muster to be at the ready to respond.

We could begin by continuing to help fill top spots in our government agencies, something at which this committee has largely done a superb job. OPM, for example, has been without a Senate confirmed Deputy Director for nearly four years. It's not that the Administration hasn't been submitting the names of qualified and talented candidates for these posts most of the time. For example, this Committee has favorably reported out the name of Navy Admiral Earl Gray, the President's nominee for this position, twice— once in 2014 and again in 2015. We need to get him confirmed so Director Archuleta has the help she needs to right the ship.

We could also build on the cyber legislation we passed last year or pass new legislation like EINSTEIN, information sharing, or data breach. We could also fully fund agency security efforts.

These are all important steps we can take, but they will incredibly difficult to accomplish if we don't work together. With that, Mr. Chairman, I thank you again for holding this hearing. I look forward to hearing from our witnesses.

###

UNITED STATES OFFICE OF PERSONNEL MANAGEMENT

**STATEMENT OF
THE HONORABLE
KATHERINE ARCHULETA
DIRECTOR
U.S. OFFICE OF PERSONNEL MANAGEMENT**

before the

**COMMITTEE ON HOMELAND SECURITY AND GOVERNMENTAL AFFAIRS
UNITED STATES SENATE**

on

"Under Attack: Federal Cybersecurity and the OPM Data Breach"

June 25, 2015

Chairman Johnson, Ranking Member Carper, and Members of the committee:

Government and non-government entities are under constant attack by evolving and advanced persistent threats and criminal actors. These adversaries are sophisticated, well-funded, and focused. Unfortunately, these attacks will not stop – if anything, they will increase. Although OPM has taken significant steps to meet our responsibility to secure the personal data of those we serve, it is clear that OPM needs to dramatically accelerate these efforts, not only for those individuals personally, but also as a matter of national security. When I was sworn in as the Director of the U.S. Office of Personnel Management (OPM) 18 months ago, I immediately became aware of security vulnerabilities in the agency's aging legacy systems and I made the modernization and security of our network and its systems one of my top priorities. My goal as Director of OPM, as laid out in OPM's February 2014 *Strategic Information Technology (IT) Plan*, has been to leverage cybersecurity best practices to protect the sensitive information entrusted to the agency, while modernizing our IT infrastructure to better confront emerging threats and meeting our mission and customer service expectations.

Statement of The Honorable Katherine Archuleta
U.S. Office of Personnel Management

June 25, 2015

Strengthening OPM's IT Security

First, I would like to address confusion regarding the number of people affected by the two recent, related cyber incidents at OPM.

It is my responsibility to provide as accurate information as I can to Congress, the public, and most importantly, the affected individuals. Second, because this information and its potential misuse concerns their lives, it is essential to identify the affected individuals as quickly as possible. Third, we face challenges in analyzing the data due to the form of the records and the way they are stored. As such, I have deployed a dedicated team to undertake this time consuming analysis and instructed them to make sure their work is accurate and completed as quickly as possible. As much as I want to have all the answers today, I do not want to be in a position of providing you or the affected individuals with potentially inaccurate data.

With these considerations in mind, I want to clarify some of the reports that have appeared in the press. Some press accounts have suggested that the number of affected individuals has expanded from 4 million individuals to 18 million individuals. Other press accounts have asserted that 4 million individuals have been affected in the personnel file incident and 18 million individuals have been affected in the background investigation incident.

Therefore, I am providing the status as we know it today and reaffirming my commitment to providing more information as soon as we know it.

First, the two kinds of data I am addressing - - personnel records and background investigations - - were affected in two different systems in two recent incidents.

Second, the number of individuals with data compromised from the personnel records incident is approximately 4.2 million, as we reported on June 4. This number has not changed, and we have notified these individuals.

Third, as I have noted, we continue to analyze the background investigation data as rapidly as possible to best understand what was compromised, and we are not at a point where we are able to provide a more definitive report on this issue.

That said, I want to address the figure of 18 million individuals that has been cited in the press. It is my understanding that the 18 million refers to a preliminary, unverified and approximate number of unique social security numbers in the background investigations data. It is not a number that I feel comfortable, at this time, represents the total number of affected individuals. The social security number portion of the analysis is still under active review, and we do not have a more definitive number. Also, there may be overlap between the individuals affected in the background investigation incident and the personnel file incident. Additionally, we are working deliberately to determine if individuals who have not had their social security numbers compromised, but may have other information exposed, should be considered individuals affected by this incident. For these reasons, the 18 million figure may change. My team is conducting this further analysis with all due speed and care, and again, I look forward to providing an accurate and complete response as soon as possible.

I also want to share with this committee some new steps that I am taking. First, I will be hiring a new cybersecurity advisor that will report directly to me. This cybersecurity advisor will work with OPM's CIO to manage ongoing response to the recent incidents, complete development of OPM's plan to mitigate future incidents, and assess whether long-term changes to OPM's IT architecture are needed to ensure that its assets are secure. I expect this individual to be serving the agency by August 1. Second, to ensure that the agency is leveraging private sector best practices and expertise, I am reaching out to Chief Information Security Officers at leading private sector companies that experience their own significant cybersecurity challenges and I will host a meeting with these experts in the coming weeks to help identify further steps the agency can take to protect its systems and information. As you know, the public and private sector both face these challenges, and we should face them together.

In March 2014, we released our *Strategic Information Technology Plan* to modernize and secure OPM's aging legacy system. The focus of the Plan is a set of strategic initiatives that will allow OPM to administer IT with greater efficiency, effectiveness, and security. This work recognizes recommendations from the U.S. Government Accountability Office and OPM's Office of Inspector General (OIG). Work to implement the Plan began immediately, and in Fiscal Years (FY) 2014 and 2015 we re-prioritized critical resources to direct nearly $70 million toward the implementation of tough new security controls to better protect our systems. OPM is also in the process of developing a new network infrastructure environment to improve the security of OPM infrastructure and IT systems. Once completed, OPM IT systems will be migrated into this new environment from the current legacy networks.

Statement of The Honorable Katherine Archuleta
U.S. Office of Personnel Management

June 25, 2015

Many of the improvements have been to address critical immediate needs, such as the security vulnerabilities in our network. These upgrades include the installation of additional firewalls; restriction of remote access without two-factor authentication; continuous monitoring of all connections to ensure that only legitimate connections have access; and deploying anti-malware software across the environment to protect and prevent the deployment or execution of cyber-crime tools that could compromise our networks. These improvements led us to the discovery of the malicious activity that had occurred, and we were able to immediately share the information so that other agencies could protect their networks.

OPM thwarts millions of intrusion attempts on its networks in an average month. We are working around the clock to identify and mitigate security weaknesses. The reality is that integrating comprehensive security technologies into large, complex outdated IT systems is a lengthy and resource-intensive effort. It is a challenging reality, but one that we are determined to address. We have implemented these tools to the maximum extent possible, but the fact is that we were not able to deploy them before these two sophisticated incidents, and, even if we had been, no single system is immune to these types of attacks.

As we address critical immediate needs we also need to continue our work to improve long-term strategic challenges that affect our ability to ensure the security of our networks. I view the relationship that OPM has with our Inspector General as collaborative. We appreciate their recommendations and take them very seriously. As our OIG has noted, OPM has been challenged for several years in building and maintaining a strong management structure and the processes needed for a successful information technology security program. OPM agrees with this assessment and it is this weakness that the Strategic IT Plan was developed to resolve.

I also want to discuss the important issue of data encryption. Though data encryption is a valuable protection method, today's adversaries are sophisticated enough that encryption alone does not guarantee protection. OPM does currently utilize encryption when possible; however, due to the age of some of our legacy systems, data encryption is not always possible. In fact, I have been advised by security experts that encryption in this instance would not have prevented the theft of this data, because the malicious actors were able to steal privileged user credentials and could decrypt the data. Our IT security team is actively building

Statement of The Honorable Katherine Archuleta
U.S. Office of Personnel Management

June 25, 2015

new systems with technology that will allow OPM not only to better identify intrusions, but to encrypt even more of our data. Currently, we are increasing the types of methods utilized to encrypt our data.

In addition to new policies that were already being implemented to centralize IT security duties under the Chief Information Officer (CIO) and to improve oversight of new major systems development, the Plan recognized that further progress was needed. Thanks to OPM CIO Donna Seymour's leadership, the OIG's November 2014 audit credited OPM for progress in bolstering information technology security policies and procedures, and for committing critical resources to the effort.

Where the audit found weaknesses in Information Security Governance and Security Assessment and Authorization, OPM was already planning and implementing upgrades that emphasized improved security and the adoption of state of the art security protocols. Once these upgrades reached a mature stage in the spring of 2015, we were able to detect earlier intrusions into our data. Cybersecurity is fundamentally about risk management, and we must ensure that any recommendation helps us achieve the most effective level of cybersecurity and at the same time, allows us to continue providing critical services to the Federal workforce.

With regard to Information Security Governance, the OIG noted that OPM had implemented significant positive changes and removed its designation as a material weakness. This was encouraging, as IT governance is a pillar of the Strategic IT Plan. An enhanced IT governance capacity will identify and ensure we fund IT investments that are more tightly aligned with our needs. It will also allow us to manage, evaluate, measure, and monitor IT services in a more consistent and repeatable manner.

Regarding the weaknesses found with Security Assessment and Authorization, the OIG had recommended that I consider shutting down 11 out of 47 of OPM's IT systems because they did not have a current and valid Authorization. I am the leader of an organization that provides critical services to over two million current Federal employees around the world. The legacy systems that we are aggressively updating are critical to the provision of those services. Shutting down systems would mean that retirees would not get paid, and that new security clearances could not be issued. I am dedicated to ensuring that OPM does everything in its power to protect the federal workforce. But part of that included ensuring that our

58

retirees receive the benefits they have earned and federal employees get the healthcare they need.

Of the systems raised in the FY 2014 audit report, eleven of those systems were expired. Of those, one, a contractor system, is presently expired. All other systems raised in the FY 2014 audit report have been either extended or provided a limited Authorization.

Addressing Federal Employees' Needs

For those approximately 4 million current and former Federal civilian employees who were potentially affected by the incident announced on June 4 regarding personnel information, OPM is offering credit monitoring services and identity theft insurance with CSID, a company that specializes in identity theft protection and fraud resolution. This comprehensive, 18-month membership includes credit report access, credit monitoring, identity theft insurance, and recovery services and is available immediately at no cost to affected individuals identified by OPM.

The high volume of notifications sent on the 18th and 19th of June, along with the a significant number of calls being made to the CSID call center from individuals who have not been impacted or notified of impact, caused wait times to increase, and those selecting on-line sign up at the end of last week experienced the CSID site timing out.

Our team is continuing to work with CSID to make the online signup experience quicker and to reduce call center wait times. These actions involve expanded staffing and call center hours, and increasing server capacity to better handle on-line sign ups at peak times. We continue to update our FAQ's on opm.gov to address questions that we are getting from individuals who have or feel they may have been impacted.

Conclusion

The OIG's assessments of OPM's plans reflected the difficulties involved in working with complex legacy systems. This type of assessment is helpful to ensure OPM has the best, most comprehensive plans possible, and the OIG report helps everyone, including Congress, understand that these are complex issues that will require significant resources, both time and funding, to correct.

Statement of The Honorable Katherine Archuleta
U.S. Office of Personnel Management

June 25, 2015

I would like to emphasize again that OPM has taken steps to ensure that greater restrictions are in place, even for privileged users. This includes removing remote access for privileged users and requiring two-factor authentication. We are looking into further protections, such as tools that mask and redact data that would not be necessary for a privileged user to see.

Thank you for this opportunity to testify today and I am happy to address any questions you may have.

U.S. Office of Personnel Management

Actions to Strengthen Cybersecurity and Protect Critical IT Systems

June 2015

I. Introduction

The recent intrusions into U.S. Office of Personnel Management (OPM) systems that house personnel and background investigation data for Federal employees and other individuals have raised questions about the security of OPM data and the integrity of its Information Technology (IT) assets. Since Director Archuleta arrived at OPM, she has led the agency in taking significant strides to enhance cybersecurity and modernize its IT systems – strides that are in many ways forging new territory and laying groundwork for the rest of government. But recently discovered incidents have underscored the fact that there is clearly more that can and must be done. Government and non-government entities are under constant attack by evolving, advanced, and persistent threats and criminal actors. These adversaries are sophisticated, well-funded, and focused. For that reason, efforts to combat them and improve Federal IT and data security must be constantly improving as well.

The following report provides a summary of the actions OPM has taken, those that are currently underway, and those that are planned for the future in order to meet this challenge. Many of these actions are based on recommendations that have been provided by independent experts such as the agency's Inspector General (IG), the Government Accountability Office (GAO), and other Federal partners. In the coming weeks and months, the agency will continue to consult with Congress, the IG, independent experts inside and outside of government, and others to identify further actions to strengthen cybersecurity and protect its critical IT systems.

II. Prior and Ongoing Actions to Improve IT System Security

Upon Director Archuleta's arrival, OPM engaged in an end-to-end review of its IT systems and processes. Based on that review, the agency developed a *Strategic Plan for Information Technology* to guide its efforts to protect its legacy systems to the maximum extent possible as it replaced them with more modern and secure systems. This plan laid out a multi-phase strategy to bolster security through realignment of professional staff, adherence to relevant laws, policies and best practices, and investments in modern tools. As Director Archuleta stated upon publication:

> "[The plan] provides a framework that is rooted in the use of human resources (HR) data throughout a lifecycle ("strategy to separation"), allowing for reuse of that data in our HR systems to support agile HR policies; establishes enabling successful practices and initiatives, and enterprise and business initiatives that define OPM's IT modernization efforts; and creates a flexible and sustainable Chief Information Officer (CIO) organization led by a strong senior executive with Federal experience in information technology, program management, and HR policy."

One of the principal elements of the plan was information security – to ensure the agency protects the identity and privacy of citizens and employees by implementing and actively monitoring standard security controls in IT systems that effectively protect the large volume of sensitive personal data collected and stored by OPM IT systems.

Under Director Archuleta's leadership, OPM has made good on that commitment by taking 23 concrete steps to improve information security:

Improving Security

1. **Implemented two factor Strong Authentication** for all privileged users, and increased the percentage of unprivileged users with two factor Strong Authentication. Requiring the utilization of a Personal Identity Verification (PIV) card or alternative form of multi-factor authentication can significantly reduce the risk of adversaries penetrating Federal networks and systems. OPM has been a leader for the Federal government in this area.
2. **Restricted remote access** for network administrators and restricted network administration functions that can be performed remotely.
3. **Reviewed all connections** to ensure that only legitimate business connections have access to the Internet.
4. **Deployed new hardware and software tools,** including 14 essential tools to secure the network. OPM continues to deploy additional security tools to improve its cybersecurity posture, including tools that mask and redact data.
5. **Deployed anti-malware software** across the environment to protect and prevent the deployment or execution of cybercrime tools that could compromise the agency's networks.
6. **Upgraded Security Assessment and Authorization** for multiple systems.
7. **Established a 24/7 Security Operations Center,** staffed by certified professionals, to monitor the network for security alerts.
8. **Implemented continuous monitoring** to enhance the ability to identify and respond, in real time or near real time, to cyber threats.
9. **Installed more firewalls** that allow the agency to filter network traffic.
10. **Centralized security management and accountability** into the Office of the CIO and staffed it with security professionals who are fully trained and dedicated to information security on a full-time basis.
11. **Conducted a comprehensive review** of IT security clauses in contracts to ensure that the appropriate oversight and protocols are in place.
12. **Developed a Risk Executive Function** to ensure risk mitigation at the organizational, business process, and information system levels, including development of Risk Executive Charter and Risk Registry Template
13. **Mandated cybersecurity awareness training** for the entire workforce.

Leveraging Outside Expertise

14. **Collaborated with agency partners** such as the Office of Management and Budget (OMB) and the National Institute of Standards and Technology to share, learn and standardize best practices, and to ensure information security policies are rigorous and cost-effective based on a risk assessment methodology that considers both current and potential threats.

15. **Worked with the intelligence community** and other stakeholders to identify high value cyber targets within the OPM network where bulk PII data are present, and mitigate the vulnerabilities of those targets to the extent practicable.
16. **Worked with law enforcement and other agencies** to shore up existing security protocols, enhance the security of its systems and detect and thwart evolving and persistent threats.
17. **Bringing in management and technology expertise** by adding experts from around the Government to help manage its incident response , provide advice on further actions, and ensure that Congress and the public are kept fully up-to-date on ongoing efforts.
18. **Helping other agencies hire IT leaders** to ensure they can acquire the personnel needed to combat evolving cyber threats. This includes leveraging tools and flexibilities such as direct hiring, excepted service hiring flexibilities and critical pay authority to bring IT and cyber experts from the private sector into the Federal government quickly and efficiently.

Modernizing Systems

19. **Invested in network remediation and stabilization** to modernize OPM's IT footprint. From Fiscal Year 2014 to 2015, OPM nearly tripled its investment in the IT modernization effort, from $31 million to $87 million. The President's 2016 Budget calls for an additional $21 million to further this effort. These funds would pay for maintenance of a sustained security operations center (SOC) to provide critical oversight of OPM's security posture and real-time 24/7 monitoring of network servers to detect and respond to malicious activity. Further, this funding includes support for stronger firewalls and storage devices for capturing security log information used for analysis in incident response
20. **Standardized operating systems.** In alignment with an IG recommendation OPM will continue standardizing operating systems and applications throughout the OPM environment, with the ultimate goal of implementing configuration baselines for all operating platforms in use by OPM. Once these baselines are in place, OPM will conduct routine compliance scans against them to identify any security vulnerabilities that may exist.

Accountability

21. **Strengthened oversight of contractors.** In alignment with recommendations made by the GAO, OPM is in the process of developing, documenting, and implementing enhanced oversight procedures for ensuring that a system test is fully executed for each contractor-operated system. These procedures will expand the policy for oversight of contractor systems currently in OPM's IT Security and Privacy Handbook.
22. **Tightened policies and practices for privileged users.** Consistent with guidance from OMB, OPM is reviewing the number of privileged users, and taking steps to minimize their numbers, limit functions that they can perform, limit the duration of time they can be logged in, limit the functions that can performed remotely, and log all privileged user activity. This review – to be conducted by the CIO and the new cybersecurity advisor – will be completed and will provide recommendations to the Director by July 15.
23. **Improved Portfolio Management** by hiring a dedicated Level 3 IT portfolio manager, as recommended by the IG, in December 2014 to lead its IT transformation efforts and ensure that security and performance requirements are addressed across the enterprise.

These actions have put OPM in a much stronger and more secure posture than it was, when Director Archuleta assumed her role. OPM systems currently thwart the millions of intrusion attempts that target its networks every month.

Moreover, it was because of the very cybersecurity enhancements described above that OPM was able to detect the sophisticated malicious activity on its network responsible for the recent incidents described below.

III.   New Actions to Bolster Security and Modernize IT Systems

The interagency incident response team has reviewed OPM's systems and concluded that there is no evidence that the intruder remains active on those systems. Yet simply because there is no evidence that this particular threat remains active does not mean that we can decrease our vigilance. And in fact, OPM is doing just the opposite.

As discussed above, OPM has already taken a number of aggressive steps over the past 18 months to increase its cybersecurity capabilities and modernize its critical IT systems. But there is clearly more that can and must be done to meet evolving cyber threats. With that in mind, OPM is taking the following **15 new actions**. Director Archuleta has directed that these actions be carried out with all due speed, as further steps to protect the critical assets and data OPM is entrusted with are of the utmost urgency.

Improving Security

1. **Completing deployment of two factor authentication** – While OPM has implemented two factor Strong Authentication (through the use of smart card log in) for all privileged users, it continues to implement this process for unprivileged users. As of the end of the second quarter of Fiscal Year 2015, nearly half of unprivileged users were using two factor authentication. Director Archuleta has directed that the agency accelerate its migration to full two factor authentication, and that this process be completed – with all users migrated to smart card log in – by August 1.
2. **Expanding continuous monitoring** – OPM is working with the Department of Homeland Security (DHS) to implement the Continuous Diagnostics and Mitigation program by March 2016. OPM will aggressively work with DHS to accelerate this schedule. OPM will also mandate continuous monitoring of contractor systems where feasible.
3. **Ensuring access to contractor systems** – OPM will establish requirements for future contracts, as appropriate, to ensure access to contractor systems in the event of an incident. This will ensure that OPM and law enforcement agencies can access data and conduct effective and immediate response in the case of any future cyber incidents. OPM will also consider whether any additional authorities from Congress are needed in order to enforce such access.
4. **Reviewing encryption of databases** – As Director Archuleta has stated, full encryption of the databases that were accessed in the recent incidents would not have been feasible, as many of OPM's systems would not have worked if they were encrypted. Moreover, encryption

would not have kept out these particular actors. That said, encryption can be a valuable tool in the agency's overall cybersecurity strategy, as emphasized by multiple members of Congress in recent hearings. Accordingly, Director Archuleta has directed a review of all agency databases to determine if there are any instances where encryption is possible but is not currently in place – and if any such instances are found, to proceed with encryption of the data. The Director has directed this review be completed by July 15.

Leveraging Outside Expertise

5. **Hiring a new cybersecurity advisor** – Director Archuleta will hire a leading cybersecurity expert from outside of government who will report directly to her. This cybersecurity advisor will work with OPM's CIO to manage ongoing response to the recent incidents, complete development of OPM's plan to mitigate future incidents, and assess whether long-term changes to OPM's IT architecture are needed to ensure that its assets are secure. OPM expects this individual to be serving the agency by August 1.

6. **Consulting with outside technology and cybersecurity experts** – To ensure that the agency is leveraging private sector best practices and expertise, Director Archuleta has reached out to Chief Information Security Officers at leading private sector companies that experience their own significant cybersecurity challenges. OPM will be holding a workshop with these experts in the coming weeks to help identify further steps the agency can take to protect its systems and information.

7. **Increasing consultation with the Inspector General** – As OPM has embarked on its IT modernization effort, it has received and addressed recommendations from the IG at multiple points. To ensure that this collaborative work continues, Director Archuleta will meet with the IG on a bi-weekly basis to receive regular advice and counsel

Modernizing Systems

8. **Migrating to a new IT environment** – OPM is incrementally engineering a modern network capable of significantly increased security controls. This new network infrastructure environment, known as the Shell, will improve the security of OPM infrastructure and IT systems. Once the Shell is implemented, OPM IT systems will be migrated into this new environment from the current legacy Local Area Network/Wide Area Network (LAN/WAN). This process will adhere to the OPM Systems Development Life Cycle, derived from Federal standards to manage OCIO Portfolios, Programs and Projects.

9. **Finalizing the scope of the migration process** – In alignment with recommendations of the Inspector General, OPM will complete an assessment of the scope of its IT modernization process before the end of the fiscal year. As part of this – and as recommended by the IG – OPM will assess the level of effort and estimated costs of the migration process. OPM will continue to track, document, and justify any changes should those estimated costs need to change.

10. **Evaluating all contracting options** – In alignment with another recommendation of the IG, as OPM considers the appropriate avenues for the Mitigation and Cleanup phases of the infrastructure improvement process, it will conduct a thorough analysis on the most reasonable and appropriate course of action, and explore all available contracting avenues

to determine the best option for the health of its modernization project and for the taxpayer.

11. **Calling on Congress for additional support** – In addition to the proposal put forth in the President's Budget, OPM has conducted a review to identify areas where additional funding would help accelerate the process of improving its systems. In doing so, the agency is identifying recommended enhancements that would accelerate its overall modernization project plan. OPM will be providing further detail on these proposed enhancements to the House and Senate appropriations committees by June 26.

Accountability

12. **Senior leadership accountability** – Director Archuleta will initiate monthly reviews with the CIO and new cybersecurity advisor of the agency's IT modernization and information security efforts to ensure continued progress and accountability.

13. **Establishing regular employee and contractor training** – As discussed above, OPM has already conducted cybersecurity awareness training for all of its employees. Given the recent incidents, OPM will be refreshing this training for all employees and contractors handling sensitive information on appropriate cyber hygiene and practices, to ensure that every individual is doing their part to protect the agency's sensitive data. Going forward, this training will be required on a bi-annual basis.

14. **Documenting incident response procedures** – While no two cyber incidents are exactly the same, agencies should have in place clear protocols and plans of actions prepared in advance to manage incident response. OPM will document Standard Operating Procedures for how it will work with other Federal partners in the event of any future incidents. It will share these procedures with the IG to solicit feedback and advice.

15. **Ensuring compliance with the Federal Information Security Management Act (FISMA)** – As recommended by the IG, OPM will modify the performance standards of all OPM system owners to require and monitor FISMA compliance for each of the information systems under their purview.

IV. Conclusion

OPM stores more Personally Identifiable Information (PII) and other sensitive records than almost any other Federal agency. This is a tremendous trust placed in the agency by the millions of current and former Federal employees, and one that OPM must continually earn through constant vigilance.

The recent breaches of OPM data make clear that cybersecurity must remain a priority for all agencies, but especially OPM. As President Obama has said, "Both state and non-state actors are sending everything they've got at trying to breach these systems...And this problem is not going to go away. It is going to accelerate. And that means that we have to be as nimble, as aggressive, and as well-resourced as those who are trying to break into these systems."

Over the past 18 months, OPM has taken aggressive steps to improve security protocols, set up continuous monitoring of its systems, establish a centralized Security Operations Center, and other measures. These steps have established a firm foundation on which OPM will continue a steadfast and unyielding effort to position the agency as a leader in Federal cybersecurity. And in fact, they led directly to uncovering the recent incidents described in this report. Without the steps, malicious actors would like continue to be actively in its systems.

The persistent and continuing attacks by malicious actors make it clear OPM must remain vigilant. That is why Director Archuleta has directed the 15 new actions described above. OPM will carry out these actions without delay. In addition, OPM is calling on Congress to take swift action to assist in this effort by providing additional resources to modernize OPM's IT systems and ensure continued appropriate oversight of the agency and its contractors.

In a world of evolving threats, there is no such thing as "total cybersecurity." But the actions outlined above, and continued collaboration with Federal partners, Congress, and outside experts will ensure that OPM has all the tools it needs to safeguard its systems and protect the men and women that serve the Federal government.

EXECUTIVE OFFICE OF THE PRESIDENT
OFFICE OF MANAGEMENT AND BUDGET
WASHINGTON, D.C. 20503
www.whitehouse.gov/omb

TESTIMONY OF TONY SCOTT
UNITED STATES CHIEF INFORMATION OFFICER
OFFICE OF MANAGEMENT AND BUDGET
BEFORE THE HOMELAND SECURITY AND GOVERNMENTAL AFFAIRS
COMMITTEE
UNITED STATES SENATE

June 25, 2015

Chairman Johnson, Ranking Member Carper, members of the Committee, thank you for the opportunity to appear before you today. I appreciate the opportunity to speak with you about recent cyber incidents impacting Federal agencies.

I would like to start by highlighting a very important point of which you are already aware: both state and non-state actors who are well financed, highly motivated are persistently attempting to breach both government and non-government systems. And these attempts are not going away. They will continue to accelerate on two dimensions: first, the attack will continue becoming more sophisticated, and secondly, as we remediate and strengthen our own practices, our detection capabilities will improve. That means that we have to be as nimble, as aggressive, and as well-resourced as those who are trying to break into our systems.

Confronting cybersecurity threats on a continuous basis is our nation's new reality– a reality that I faced in the private sector, and am continuing to see here in my new role as the Federal Chief Information Officer (CIO). As Federal CIO, I lead the Office of Management and Budget's (OMB) Office of E-Government & Information Technology (IT) (E-Gov). My office is responsible for developing and overseeing the implementation of Federal Information Technology policy. Even though my team has a variety of responsibilities, I will focus today's remarks on cybersecurity.

OMB's Role in Federal Cybersecurity

Under the Federal Information Security Modernization Act of 2014 (FISMA), OMB is responsible for federal information security oversight and policy issuance. OMB executes its responsibilities in close coordination with its Federal cybersecurity partners, including the Department of Homeland Security (DHS) and the Department of Commerce's National Institute of Standards and Technology (NIST).

Additionally, OMB recently announced the creation of a dedicated cybersecurity unit within the Office of E-Gov & IT: the E-Gov Cyber and National Security Unit (E-Gov Cyber). The creation of the E-Gov Cyber Unit reflects OMB's focus on conducting robust, data-driven oversight of agencies' cybersecurity programs, monitoring and improving responses to major cyber security incidents, and issuing Federal guidance consistent with emerging technologies and risks.

This is the team behind the work articulated in the Fiscal Year (FY) 2014 FISMA report which highlighted both successes and challenges facing Federal agencies' cyber programs. In FY 2015, the E-Gov Cyber Unit is targeting oversight through CyberStat reviews, prioritizing agencies with high risk factors as determined by cybersecurity performance and incident data. Additionally, the Unit is driving FISMA implementation by providing agencies with the guidance they need in this dynamic environment. The top FY 2015 policy priority of the team is updating Circular A-130, which is the central government-wide policy document that establishes agency guidelines on how to manage information resources, including best practices for how to secure those resources.

Recent Cyber Incidents Affecting the Office of Personnel Management (OPM)

My colleagues will fully address the recent cyber incidents affecting the Office of Personnel Management (OPM). In terms of the role of OMB in responding to recent events, my office monitors very closely all reports of incidents affecting federal networks and systems. We use these reports to look for trends and patterns as well as for areas where our government-wide processes, policies, and other practices can be strengthened. We then update our guidance and coordinate with other agencies to ensure that guidance is implemented. And thanks to the good work done by this committee last Congressional sessions, the recently passed Federal Information Technology Acquisition Reform Act (FITARA) and our guidance associated with the legislation strengthens the role of the CIO in agency cybersecurity.

In this case, OPM notified OMB in April 2015 of an incident affecting data in transit in its network. OPM reported that they were working closely with various government agencies on a comprehensive investigation and response to this incident. We have been actively monitoring the situation and have been engaged in making sure that there is a government-wide response to the events at OPM.

Strengthening Federal Cyber Security Practices

To further improve Federal cyber infrastructure and protect systems against these evolving threats, last week OMB launched a 30-day Cybersecurity Sprint. The team is comprised of the Office of Management and Budget's (OMB) E-Gov Cyber and National Security Unit (E-Gov Cyber), the National Security Council Cybersecurity Directorate (NSC Cyber), the Department of Homeland Security (DHS), the Department of Defense (DOD), and other agencies. At the end of the review, the Government will create and operationalize a set of action plans and strategies to further address critical cybersecurity priorities and recommend a *Federal Civilian Cybersecurity Strategy*. This strategy will detail short, medium and long term steps that the Government should take to address current operational deficiencies and vulnerabilities as well as future care of our Federal IT infrastructure.

<u>Key principles of the *Strategy* will include</u>:

- *Protecting Data*: Better protect data at rest and in transit.
- *Improving Situational Awareness*: Improve indication and warning.
- *Increasing Cybersecurity Proficiency*: Ensure a robust capacity to recruit and retain cybersecurity personnel.
- *Increase Awareness*: improve overall risk awareness by all users.
- *Standardizing and Automating Processes*: Decrease time needed to manage configurations and patch vulnerabilities.
- *Controlling, Containing, and Recovering from Incidents*: Contain malware proliferation, privilege escalation, and lateral movement. Quickly identify and resolve events and incidents.
- *Strengthening Systems Lifecycle Security*: Increase inherent security of platforms by buying more secure systems and retiring legacy systems in a timely manner.
- *Reducing Attack Surfaces*: Decrease complexity and number of things defenders need to protect.

As part of the effort, OMB instructed Federal agencies to immediately take a number of steps to protect Federal information and assets and improve the resilience of Federal networks.

Specifically, Federal agencies must:

- Immediately deploy indicators provided by DHS regarding priority threat-actor techniques, tactics, and procedures to scan systems and check logs.
- Patch critical vulnerabilities without delay and report to OMB and DHS on progress and challenges within 30 days.
- Tighten policies and practices for privileged users.
- Dramatically accelerate implementation of multi-factor authentication, especially for privileged users.

Summary

In closing, I want to underscore a critical point I made at the beginning of this testimony: both state and non-state actors are attempting to breach both government and non-government systems. And this problem is not going to go away. It's going to accelerate. Ensuring the security of information within the Federal government's networks and systems will remain a core focus of the Administration as we move aggressively to implement innovative protections and respond quickly to new challenges as they arise. In addition to the actions we are taking, we also look forward to working with Congress on legislative actions that may further protect our nation's critical networks and systems. Providing Departments and Agencies with the proper legal authority along with the requisite funding are key steps to ensuring that our Federal civilian networks are adequately protected. I encourage you to continue working with the administration to move important, necessary cybersecurity legislation through Congress.

I thank the Committee for holding this hearing, and for your commitment to improving Federal cybersecurity. I would be pleased to answer any questions you may have.

Written Testimony

of

Dr. Andy Ozment

Assistant Secretary for Cybersecurity and Communications

U.S. Department of Homeland Security

Before the

U.S. Senate

Committee on Homeland Security and Government Affairs

Regarding

The OPM Compromise and the DHS Role in Federal Cybersecurity

Introduction

Chairman Johnson, Ranking Member Carper, and members of the Committee, thank you for the opportunity to appear before you today. The Office of Personnel Management (OPM) compromise clearly demonstrates the challenge facing the federal government in protecting our citizens' and employees' personal information against sophisticated, agile, and persistent threats. Addressing these threats is a shared responsibility. I will discuss the Department's role in the recent compromise at OPM and how we are working with OPM and other agencies to accelerate improved cybersecurity across the Federal Government.

The Role of the Department of Homeland Security in Federal Cybersecurity

Cyber security, like physical security, requires layers of protections. The *Federal Information Security Modernization Act of 2014* specifies that federal agencies are responsible for their own cybersecurity. Although agencies must take the lead in their own cybersecurity, as OPM is currently doing, DHS has the mission to provide a common baseline of security across the civilian government and help agencies manage their cyber risk. DHS, through its National Protection and Programs Directorate (NPPD), assists agencies by providing this baseline for the federal government through the EINSTEIN and Continuous Diagnostics and Mitigation (CDM) programs, by measuring and motivating agencies to implement best practices, by serving as a hub for information sharing, and by providing incident response assistance when agencies suffer a cyber-intrusion.

Like cameras, alarms, and fences around a physical building, EINSTEIN protects agencies' unclassified networks at the perimeter of each agency. Furthermore, EINSTEIN provides situational awareness across the government, as threats detected in one agency are shared with all others so they can take appropriate protective action. The U.S. Government could not achieve such situational awareness through individual agency efforts alone.

The first two versions of EINSTEIN – EINSTEIN 1 and 2 – identify abnormal network traffic patterns and detect known malicious traffic. This capability is fully deployed and screening all Federal civilian traffic that is routed through a Trusted Internet Connection (a secure gateway between each agency's internal network and the Internet). EINSTEIN 3 Accelerated (EINSTEIN 3A), which actively blocks known malicious traffic, is currently being deployed through the primary Internet Service Providers serving the Federal government. EINSTEIN 1 and 2 use only unclassified information, while EINSTEIN 3A uses classified information. Using classified indicators allows EINSTEIN 3A to detect and block many of the most significant cybersecurity threats. I am happy to discuss the Department's efforts to accelerate EINSTEIN 3A's deployment across the Federal civilian government, as well as the development of advanced malware and behavioral analysis capabilities that will automatically identify and separate suspicious traffic for further inspection, even if the precise indicator has not been seen before. We are examining best-in-class technologies from the private sector to evolve to this next stage of network defense. As I will discuss later, EINSTEIN played a key role in understanding the recent compromise at OPM.

Continuous Diagnostics and Mitigation (CDM)

Security cannot be achieved through only one type of tool. EINSTEIN is a perimeter system, but it will never be able to block every threat. It must be complemented with systems and tools inside agency networks. Through the CDM program, DHS provides federal civilian agencies with tools to monitor agencies' internal networks. I am happy to take any questions about how CDM protects networks and the role is play in cybersecurity, but first I want to address the current incident.

DHS's Role in the OPM Compromise

Breach of OPM Federal Personnel Records Stored by the Department of the Interior

Based on guidance provided by DHS in mitigating an earlier cybersecurity incident, the Office of Personnel Management (OPM) has spent the last year implementing improved cybersecurity capabilities across its networks. As a result, in April 2015, OPM became aware of a cybersecurity intrusion affecting one of its systems. As soon as OPM identified malicious activity on their network, they shared this information with the NCCIC. The NCCIC then used EINSTEIN 2 to look back in time for other compromises across the Federal civilian government. Through this process, the NCCIC identified a potential compromise at a Department of Interior data center which stored federal personnel records for OPM. Next, the NCCIC used the EINSTEIN 1 system to determine whether data exfiltration had occurred. In May, 2015, the NCCIC incident response team confirmed exfiltration of approximately 4.2 million federal personnel records stored at the DOI data center on behalf of OPM. NCCIC assesses that the adversary was present in the applicable DOI data center from October 2014 to March 2015.

Breach of OPM Background Investigation Records Stored by OPM Itself

In May 2015, as a result of continuing forensic analysis of its environment, OPM identified additional malicious activity on its own network. In June 2015, the inter-agency team determined that several OPM applications related to background investigations had been exposed to the adversary. NCCIC assesses that the adversary was present on OPM's network from June 2014 to January 2015. This remains an active investigation, and DHS, the FBI, and other partners are working closely with OPM to determine the extent of compromised background investigation information and potential implications. Information regarding this incident may change as the investigation progresses.

One of the important roles DHS plays is helping share information across agencies, and in some cases, with the private sector. For example, as soon as OPM identified malicious activity on their network, they shared this information with DHS. NPPD then developed a signature for the particular threat, and used EINSTEIN 2 to look back in time for other compromises across the Federal civilian government. This same threat information is used by EINSTEIN 3A to block potential threats from impacting federal networks. Thus, DHS used EINSTEIN 3A to ensure that this cyber threat could not exploit other agencies protected by the system. As noted, DHS is accelerating EINSTEIN 3A deployment across the federal government. While it is challenging to estimate the potential impact of a prevented event, each of these malicious DNS requests or emails that were blocked by EINSTEIN 3A may conceivably have led to a cybersecurity compromise of severe consequence.

DHS's Role in Federal Incident Reponses

Cybersecurity is about risk management, and we cannot eliminate all risk. Agencies that implement best practices and share information will increase the cost for adversaries and stop many threats. But ultimately, there exists no perfect cyber defense, and persistent adversaries will find ways to infiltrate networks in both government and the private sector. When an incident does occur, the NCCIC offers on-site assistance to find the adversary, drive them out, and restore service. In Fiscal Year 2015, the NCCIC has already provided onsite incident response to 32 incidents – nearly double the total in all of Fiscal Year 2014. The NCCIC also coordinates responses to significant incidents to give senior leaders a clear understanding of the situation and give operators the information they need to respond effectively. Similar to the recent incident at OPM, providing on-site incident response assistance also allows the NCCIC to identify indicators of compromise that can then be shared with other agencies and applied to EINSTEIN for broad protection across the federal government.

Cybersecurity Legislation

Last year, Congress acted in a bipartisan manner to pass critical cybersecurity legislation that enhanced DHS's ability to work with the private sector and other Federal civilian departments in each of their own cybersecurity activities, and enhanced the Department's cyber workforce authorities. As I noted, DHS is using the authority granted in one of those bills – the *Federal Information Security Modernization Act of 2014* – to direct Federal civilian Executive branch agencies to fix critical vulnerabilities on their Internet-facing devices through the recent issuance of a Binding Operational Directive.

Additional legislation is needed. I previously highlighted EINSTEIN's key role in identifying and mitigating an additional potential compromise during the OPM activity. The Department and Administration have a long-standing request of Congress to remove obstacles to the EINSTEIN program's deployment across Federal civilian agency information systems by codifying the program's authorities and resolving lingering concerns among certain agencies. Some agencies have questioned how deployment of EINSTEIN under DHS authority relates to their existing statutory restrictions on the use and disclosure of agency data. DHS and the Administration are seeking statutory changes to clarify this uncertainty and to ensure agencies understand that they can disclose their network traffic to DHS for narrowly tailored purposes to protect agency networks, while making clear that privacy protections for the data will remain in place. I look forward to working with Congress to further clarify DHS's authority to rapidly and efficiently deploy this protective technology.

In addition, carefully updating laws to facilitate cybersecurity information sharing within the private sector and between the private and government sectors is also essential to improving the Nation's cybersecurity. While many companies currently share cybersecurity threat information under existing laws, there is a heightening need to increase the volume and speed of information shared without sacrificing the trust of the American people or the protection of privacy, confidentiality, civil rights, or civil liberties. It is essential to ensure that cyber threat information can be collated quickly in the NCCIC, analyzed, and shared quickly among trusted partners, including with law enforcement, so that network owners and operators can take necessary steps to block threats and avoid damage.

Conclusion

Federal agencies are a rich target and will continue to experience frequent attempted intrusions. This problem is not unique to the government – it is shared across a global cybersecurity community. The key to good cyber security is awareness and constant vigilance at machine speed. As our detection methods continue to improve, more events will come to light. The recent breach at OPM is emblematic of this trend, as OPM was able to detect the intrusion by implementing cybersecurity best practices recommended by DHS. As network defenders are able to see and thwart more events, we will inevitably identify more malicious activity and disappoint the adversary's attempts to access sensitive information and systems. We are facing a major challenge in protecting our most sensitive information against sophisticated, well-resourced, and persistent adversaries. In response, we are accelerating deployment of the tools we have and are working to bring cutting-edge capabilities online. And we are asking our partner agencies and Congress to take action and work with us to strengthen the cybersecurity of our

federal agencies.

Office of the Inspector General
United States Office of Personnel Management

Statement of the Honorable
Patrick E. McFarland
Inspector General

before the

Committee on Homeland Security and Governmental Affairs

United States Senate

on

"Under Attack: Federal Cybersecurity and the OPM Data Breach"

June 25, 2015

Chairman Johnson, Ranking Member Carper, and Members of the Committee:

Good morning. My name is Patrick E. McFarland. I am the Inspector General of the U.S. Office of Personnel Management (OPM). Thank you for inviting me to testify at today's hearing on information technology (IT) security at OPM. Today I will briefly describe our IT audit work, and then discuss a Flash Audit Alert recently issued by the Office of the Inspector General (OIG)

Legacy Systems and the Recent Security Breaches

In the past week, there have been assertions that OPM's legacy information systems are supported by very old technology (specifically COBOL, a mainframe programming language), and therefore could not be protected by modern security controls. However, we know from our audit work that some of the OPM systems involved in the data breaches run on modern operating and database management systems. Consequently, modern security technology such as encryption or data loss prevention could have been implemented on these specific systems.

Also, OPM has stated that because the agency's IT environment is based on legacy technology, it is necessary to complete a full overhaul of the existing technical infrastructure in order to address the immediate security concerns. While we agree in principle that this is an ideal future goal for the agency's IT environment, there are steps that OPM can take (or has already taken) to secure its current IT environment.

For example, OPM has significantly upgraded security controls to protect the perimeter of its network and prevent the type of attacks that occurred in 2014. In addition, some of OPM's most sensitive systems are compatible with additional security controls such as data encryption and other data loss prevention techniques, which could be utilized to protect OPM's systems. Moreover, implementing full two-factor authentication to access OPM's major IT systems will add an additional layer of defense that will go a long way toward preventing additional data breaches.

OIG's FISMA Work

In accordance with the Federal Information Security Management Act, commonly known as "FISMA," our office conducts an annual audit of OPM's IT security programs and practices. Although OPM has made progress in certain areas, some of the current problems and weaknesses were identified as far back as Fiscal Year (FY) 2007. We believe this long history of systemic failures to properly manage its IT infrastructure may have ultimately led to the breaches we are discussing today.

Today I will talk about three of the most significant concerns highlighted in our FY 2014 FISMA report. However, it is important to note that our report contained a total of 29 recommendations covering a wide variety of IT security topics. Only 3 of these 29 recommendations have been closed to date, and 9 of the open recommendations are long-standing issues that were rolled-forward from prior year FISMA audits.

1. Information Security Governance

Information security governance is the management structure and processes that form the foundation of a successful information technology security program. This is an area where OPM has seen significant improvement. However, some of the past weaknesses still haunt the agency today.

OPM's Office of the Chief Information Officer (OCIO) was responsible for the agency's overall technical infrastructure and provided boundary-level security controls for the systems residing on this infrastructure. However, each OPM program office historically had primary responsibility for managing security controls specific to its own IT systems. There was often confusion and disagreement as to which controls were the responsibility of the OCIO, and which were the responsibility of the program offices.

As a result of this decentralized governance structure, many security controls went unimplemented and/or remained untested, and OPM routinely failed a variety of FISMA metrics year after year. Therefore, we identified this security governance issue as a material weakness in all of our FISMA audits from FY 2007 through FY 2013.

However, in FY 2014, we changed the classification of this issue to a significant deficiency, which is less serious than a material weakness. This change was prompted by important improvements that were the result of changes instituted in recent years by OPM. Specifically, OPM has implemented a team of Information System Security Officers (ISSO) that report to the OCIO and who have responsibility for managing security for the agency's various information systems.

This new governance structure has resulted in improvement in the consistency and quality of security practices for the various IT systems owned by the agency.

Although we are optimistic that these improvements will continue, it is apparent that the OCIO continues to be negatively impacted by years of decentralized security governance, as the technical infrastructure remains fragmented and therefore inherently difficult to protect.

2. Security Assessment and Authorization

A Security Assessment and Authorization (Authorization) is a comprehensive process under which the IT security controls of an information system are thoroughly assessed against applicable security standards. After the assessment is complete, a formal Authorization memorandum is signed indicating that the system is cleared to operate in the agency's technical environment.

The Office of Management and Budget (OMB) mandates that all major Federal information systems have a valid Authorization (that is, that they have all been subjected to this *process*) every three years, unless a mature continuous monitoring system is in place (which OPM does not yet have). Although, as mentioned, IT security responsibility is being centralized under the OCIO, it is still the responsibility of OPM program offices to facilitate and pay for the Authorization process for the IT systems that they own.

OPM has a long history of issues related to system Authorizations. Our FY 2010 FISMA audit report contained a material weakness related to incomplete, inconsistent, and poor quality Authorization packages. This issue improved over the next two years, and was removed as an audit concern in FY 2012.

However, problems with OPM's system Authorizations have recently resurfaced. In FY 2014, 21 OPM systems were due for Authorization, but 11 of those were not completed on time and were therefore operating and continue to operate without a valid Authorization.[1] This is a drastic increase from prior years, and represents a systemic issue of inadequate planning by OPM program offices to assess and authorize the information systems that they own.

Although the majority of our FISMA audit work is performed towards the end of the fiscal year, it already appears that there will be a greater number of systems this year operating without a valid Authorization. In April, the CIO issued a memorandum that granted an extension of the previous Authorizations for all systems whose Authorization had already expired, and for those scheduled to expire through September 2016. Should this moratorium on Authorizations continue, the agency will have up to 23 systems that have not been subject to a thorough security controls assessment. The justification for this action was that OPM is in the process of modernizing its IT infrastructure and once this modernization is complete, all systems would have to receive new Authorizations anyway.

While we support the OCIO's effort to modernize its systems, this action to extend Authorizations is contrary to OMB guidance, which specifically states that an "extended" or "interim" Authorization is not valid. Consequently, these systems are still operating without a current Authorization, as they have not been subject to the complete security assessment process that the Authorization memorandum is intended to represent.

It is true that OMB now allows agencies to make ongoing Authorization decisions for IT systems based on the continuous monitoring of security controls – rather than enforcing a static, three-year re-Authorization process. However, OPM has not yet developed a mature continuous monitoring program. Until such a program is in place, we continue to expect OPM to re-authorize all of its IT systems every three years.

One effective way to reduce non-compliance with FISMA requirements would be for OPM to impose administrative sanctions on the program offices. We recommended that the performance standards of all OPM major system owners include a requirement related to FISMA compliance for the systems they own. Since OMB requires a valid Authorization for all Federal IT systems, we also recommended that the OPM Director consider shutting down systems that were in violation. None of the systems in violation were shut down.

Not only was a large volume (11 out of 47 systems) of OPM's IT systems operating without a valid Authorization, but several of these systems are among the most critical and sensitive applications owned by the agency.

Two of the OCIO systems without an Authorization are general support systems that host a variety of other major applications. Over 65 percent of all systems operated by OPM (not including contractor-operated systems) reside on one of these two support systems, and are therefore subject to any security risks that exist on the support systems.

---

[1] The OIG is the co-owner of one of these IT systems, the Audit Reports and Receivables Tracking System. This system has been reclassified as a minor system on the OPM general support system (GSS), and cannot be Authorized until the OCIO Authorizes the GSS.

Furthermore, two additional systems without Authorizations are owned by OPM's Federal Investigative Services, which is responsible for facilitating background investigations for suitability and security clearance determinations. Any weaknesses in the IT systems supporting this program office could potentially have national security implications.

As I explained, maintaining active Authorizations for all IT systems is a critical element of a Federal information security program, and failure to thoroughly assess and address a system's security weaknesses increases the risk of a security breach. We believe that the volume and sensitivity of OPM systems that are operating without an active Authorization represents a material weakness in the internal control structure of the agency's IT security program.

3. Technical Security Controls

As previously stated, our FY 2014 FISMA report contained a total of 29 audit recommendations related to a wide variety of technical controls.

There are many steps that OPM could take today to help improve the security posture of its existing technical environment. OPM has already implemented a variety of new controls and tools over the past year designed to strengthen the agency's technical infrastructure. However, in order to be effective, these tools must be installed and configured correctly, and must cover the entire technical environment. Our audit work has determined that this is not always the case.

Some of the specific technical weaknesses that we have identified include:

- Vulnerability scans – vulnerability scanning tools were not running correctly because they did not have the correct credentials, and the scans were not targeting the full environment. In addition, OPM did not have a process to track the status of vulnerabilities identified in the scans;

- System inventory – OPM has not developed a comprehensive list of minor applications that reside on the agency's general support systems. In addition, our vulnerability scan test work detected servers and databases that could not be accounted for on any system inventory;

- Personal identity verification (PIV) authentication – none of the agency's major applications require two-factor authentication via PIV credentials;

- Baseline configurations – OPM has not documented pre-approved secure configurations for the operating systems it utilizes;
- Configuration change control - OPM cannot ensure that all changes made to information systems have been properly documented and approved;

- Patch management – our vulnerability scan test work determined that numerous servers were not patched on a timely basis;

- VPN connections – VPN connections do not time out after 30 minutes of inactivity; and,

- Continuous monitoring – OPM does not have a mature continuous monitoring program and still relies on the periodic assessment of security controls.

OPM's Infrastructure Overhaul Project

In April 2014, in response to the March 2014 breach, OPM initiated a major IT overhaul. The initial plan was to make major security improvements to the existing environment and continue to operate OPM systems in their current location. During the process of implementing security upgrades, OPM determined that it would be more effective to completely overhaul the agency's IT infrastructure and architecture and move it into an entirely new environment (referred to as the Shell).

There are four phases in the Project:
- Tactical – shoring up the existing security environment
- Shell – creating the new data centers and IT architecture
- Migration – migrating all OPM systems to the new environment
- Clean-up – decommissioning existing hardware and systems

Our understanding is that the Tactical phase was completed in April 2015 and the Shell phase is underway and is expected to be completed this fall.

It is important to understand that the Tactical phase of this Project was in fact urgent, and it was absolutely critical to complete it as quickly as possible. However, the other phases of the Project are really a capital investment. These modernization efforts are indeed needed, but like any long-term investment, the Project must be carefully planned and implemented.

We support OPM's efforts to modernize and better secure its IT environment; however, we have two significant concerns with this Project, resulting in the issuance of a Flash Audit Alert.

Flash Audit Alert

The typical audit process can take up to 10 to 12 months from the start of the audit to the issuance of the final report. As part of our normal audit process, we provide a draft audit report to OPM for comment. It is a fact finding step to ensure that our audit field work is complete and accurate. We consider those comments, make any necessary changes, and incorporate them into our final audit report.

However, sometimes in the course of our work, we discover significant evidence of a critical problem that needs *immediate* attention by OPM. In those situations, we issue what is called a "Flash Audit Alert." We do not normally provide a draft of this alert to the agency for comment given the time sensitive nature of the matter.

After our auditors finished conducting their initial review of the Project, we determined (1) the situation was serious enough to issue a Flash Audit Alert and (2) because of the significance of the Project, we would provide the agency with a brief window to provide comments on the draft alert.

We provided a draft copy of our Flash Audit Alert to the Office of the Chief Information Officer (OCIO) on June 2, 2015, after verbally briefing the CIO several days before. We requested comments by June 5th, and later extended that to June 10th. By June 17th we still had not received comments, or indication that comments would be forthcoming. Because of the urgency of the situation, I issued the Flash Audit Alert without the benefit of agency comments.

The two primary concerns discussed in the Flash Audit Alert relate to (1) project management and (2) the use of a sole-source contract.

1. Project Management Activities

The most significant shortcoming of OPM's management of the Project is that it has not prepared a "Major IT Business Case" proposal (formerly known as the OMB Exhibit 300), as required by OMB for IT projects of this size and scope. Preparing an OMB proposal would require OPM to fully evaluate the costs, benefits, and risks associated with its planned Project, and present its business case to OMB to seek approval and funding.

OMB Circular A-11 Appendix 6 defines capital budgeting requirements for capital asset projects. The basic concepts are that capital asset projects require proper planning, cost/benefit analysis, financing, and risk management. This includes demonstrating that the return on investment exceeds the cost of funds used, and that the full cost of the project is appropriated before work begins. Finally, the Circular requires risk management and earned value management throughout the life-cycle of the Project to ensure that it continues to meet cost and schedule targets.

For OPM to complete this process it must first fully determine the true scope and cost of the project. However, we learned from our audit work that OPM is still evaluating its existing IT architecture, including the identification of all mainframe applications that will need to be migrated to the Shell environment. Further, other systems will need to be redesigned before they can be migrated. There are approximately 50 major IT systems in OPM's inventory, and a large number of related sub-systems. Until this evaluation is complete, OPM is not able to estimate how long it will take or how much it will cost to complete the Migration phase of the Project.

Despite this, OPM officials informed us that the Migration phase will be complete in 18 to 24 months. We believe that OPM is highly unlikely to meet this target. Many critical OPM applications (including those that process annuity payments for Federal retirees, reimburse health insurance companies for claims payments, and manage background investigations) run on OPM's mainframe computers. These applications are based on legacy technology, and will need to be completely renovated to be compatible with OPM's proposed new IT architecture.

This will be a highly complex and monumental task. OPM has a history of troubled system development projects. Despite multiple attempts OPM has failed to modernize its retirement claims processing system. Although the 2009 revamp of OPM's financial system (now called CBIS) was ultimately partially successful, it was also fraught with difficulty. The CBIS project was the main focus of agency leadership at that time. It was relatively well managed, and was subject to oversight from several independent entities, including my office, but it still required two years and over $30 million to complete.

OPM's current initiative will be far more complex than anything OPM has attempted in the past, since each individual application migration should be treated as its own project similar to these examples. Furthermore, there are many other systems besides OPM's mainframe applications that will also need to be modified to some extent to be compatible with the Shell environment.

Even more troubling is the fact that OPM has not followed basic best practices for program management including developing a project charter, a comprehensive list of stakeholders, a feasibility study and impact assessment, test plans, and other standard project management artifacts.

In addition to defining cost and schedule targets, the OMB Major IT Business Case process is intended to secure funding for major IT investments before work begins. However, OPM has already committed substantial funds toward this project without completing the process. In FY 2015 OPM has obligated approximately $32 million toward shoring up its existing IT security controls and establishing the Shell environment. In its FY 2016 budget request, OPM requested an additional $21 million from OMB for the Project.

OPM program officials told us that some of the Project's funding will come from the $21 million budget request, $5 million from the U.S. Department of Homeland Security, and from assessments on the program offices. In addition, program offices will be required to fund the migration of applications they own from their existing budgets. However, program office budgets are intended to fund OPM's core operations, not subsidize a major IT infrastructure project.

It is unlikely that OPM will be able to fund the substantial migration costs related to this Project without a significantly adverse impact on its mission unless it seeks dedicated funding through Congressional appropriation. Also, OPM's current budget approach seems to violate IT spending transparency principles promoted by OMB's budget guidance and its IT Dashboard initiative, which is intended to "shine [a] light onto the performance and spending of IT investments across the Federal Government."

Without a dedicated funding stream, there is a very high risk that funding will be inadequate to support the entire Migration phase, which is likely to be complex, time consuming, and extremely expensive. In addition, without the disciplined project management processes that are associated with the OMB Major IT Business Case process, there is a high risk that this Project will fail to meet all of its stated objectives. In this scenario, the agency would be forced to indefinitely support multiple data centers, further stretching already inadequate resources, possibly making both environments less secure, and increasing costs to taxpayers. This outcome would be contrary to the stated goals of creating a more secure IT environment at a lower cost.

The best chance for a successful modernization of OPM's IT environment is to develop and execute a comprehensive plan based on accepted project management disciplined processes.

OPM's Response to the Flash Audit Alert

OPM submitted a response to our Flash Audit Alert on June 22, 2015. First, OPM disagreed that they should follow industry best practices. OPM has its own Systems Development Life Cycle (SDLC) and the agency believes it is adhering to that policy. However, the OIG would like to point out that OPM is not complying with its own SDLC, which requires similar documentation as industry best practices.

Second, OPM implied that the agency did not need to submit a Major IT Business Case to OMB because (1) it would take too long and the Tactical phase had to be implemented quickly and (2) the agency worked closely with OMB, and thus already had OMB's approval. OPM noted that "submitting an initial Major IT Business Case document requires anywhere from eight months to a year of research, consultations, discussion, and effort." OPM repeatedly stated that it would have delayed their work to prepare this document.

Although this is indeed a time consuming process, the OIG firmly believes that work on this Project should not move forward without this kind of careful planning. Indeed, we are alarmed that the agency sees such vital planning steps (like defining the scope and costs of the entire Project) as administrative impediments to action.

Finally, OPM stated that another reason supporting not having a Major IT Business Case is that the migration of the systems are part of existing IT Investments (that is, IT projects for which a Major IT Business Case has been prepared) that are already being tracked on OMB's IT Dashboard by the program offices that own those systems.

The OIG disagrees. The OMB concept is that there should be transparency and accountability on IT projects. First, not every OPM IT system is associated with an IT Investment that is tracked on the OMB IT Dashboard. Essentially, OPM is not treating this modernization as a single project, but rather multiple projects conducted by the individual program offices. This approach prevents transparency and accountability at the agency level by having the program offices subsume the costs. This also reverses the progress OPM has made towards centralizing its IT functions within the OCIO. Under this model, no one person is accountable for the success of the Project.

2. Sole-Source Contract

OPM has secured a sole-source contract with a vendor to manage the infrastructure improvement project from start to finish. Although OPM completed a Justification for Other Than Full and Open Competition (JOFOC) to justify this contract, we do not agree that it is appropriate to use this contract for the entire Project.

The initial phase of the Project covered the procurement, installation, and configuration of a variety of software tools designed to improve the IT security posture of the agency (the Tactical phase). We agree that recent security breaches at OPM warranted a thorough and immediate reaction to secure the existing environment, and that the JOFOC was appropriate for this activity. However, we do not agree that it is appropriate to use a sole-source contract for the long-term system development and migration efforts.

OPM officials informed us that the reason for using the sole-source contract for the long-term was to ensure continuity. The OCIO believes the same vendor that helped build the infrastructure should be responsible for migrating applications into that environment.

Federal Acquisition Regulation § 6.302 outlines seven scenarios where contracting without full and open competition may be appropriate, two of which relate to an unusual and compelling urgency and national security implications. There is no exception to the requirement for full and open competition for vendor continuity for the convenience of the agency.

The current vendor may well be chosen as the successful bidder through full and open competition when the Migration and Clean-up phases begin. Without subjecting the remainder of this process to competition, there is a high risk that project costs will be inflated. Further, it is highly unlikely that any single vendor is qualified for the Migration phase. OPM's information systems are supported by a wide variety of operating systems, databases, and programming languages. Each individual application migration will likely require dedicated contractor support by a vendor that specializes in the specific technology supporting that system.

The Migration and Clean-up phases are not responses to a crisis situation, as the Tactical phase was. Therefore, we believe that OPM should subject the remainder of the project to contracting vehicles other than the sole-source contract used for the Tactical and Shell phases.

OPM's Response

In its June 22nd response to the Flash Audit Alert, OPM implies that the OIG misunderstands the scope of the contract. However, our auditors reviewed both the JOFOC and the contracts, and it is clear in the documents that OPM intends to use the sole-source contract for the full scope of the Project. Further, the CIO personally informed the OIG staff that the contract was for all four phases of the contract because continuity was important to the success of the Project. In fact, if OPM intended to have multiple contractors work on the Project, then requests for proposals (known as RFPs) for that work would already have been published, considering that the Migration phase is supposed to be completed by 2017.

Conclusion

While I fully support OPM's efforts to modernize its IT environment, I am concerned that there is a high risk that its efforts will ultimately be unsuccessful. For example, if the Migration phase fails, the results could be catastrophic. The agency could end up with half of its systems in the new Shell environment and half of its systems in the legacy environment. Neither of the environments would be fully secure, and OPM would be in a position where it is forced to pay indefinitely for the overhead costs of both infrastructures.

System development projects by their very nature are complex and prone to failure. Even with the application of strict project management techniques, many projects either fail entirely, or are only partially successful. Even so, there is a chance that this effort will ultimately succeed given time, leadership, and strong project management.

I am happy to answer any questions you may have.

Table 8: CFO Act Agencies' Scores

Agency	FY 2014 (%)	FY 2013 (%)	FY 2012 (%)
General Services Administration	99	98	99
Department of Justice	99	98	94
Department of Homeland Security	98	99	99
Nuclear Regulatory Commission	96	98	99
Social Security Administration	96	96	98
National Aeronautics and Space Administration	95	91	92
Department of the Interior	92	79	92
Department of Education	91	89	79
National Science Foundation	87	88	90
United States Agency for International Development (USAID)	86	83	66
Environmental Protection Agency	84	77	77
Department of Labor	82	76	82
Department of Veteran Affair	80	81	81
Department of Energy	78	75	72
Office of Personnel Management	74	83	77
Department of the Treasury	67	76	76
Department of Transportation	63	61	53
Small Business Administration	58	55	47
U.S. Department of Agriculture	53	37	34
Department of State	42	51	53
Department of Health and Human Services	35	43	50
Department of Housing and Urban Development	19	28	66
Department of Defense	N/A*	N/A*	N/A*
Department of Commerce	N/A†	87	61

Source: Data provided to DHS via CyberScope from November 15, 2012, to November 14, 2014
* Due to the size of the Department, the DOD OIG is unable to definitively report a yes or no answer for all FISMA attributes.
† Commerce OIG's FISMA audit scope was reduced as a result of (1) attrition of several key IT security staff, (2) the need to complete audit work assessing the security posture of key weather satellite systems that support a national critical mission, and (3) additional office priorities. As a result, the FISMA submission primarily focused on assessing policies and procedures, and covered a limited number of systems that would not warrant computation of a compliance score.

Colleen M. Kelley

National President

National Treasury Employees Union

Statement for the Record

For

Senate Committee on Homeland Security
and Governmental Affairs

"Under Attack: Federal Cybersecurity and the Office of
Personnel Management Data Breach"

June 25, 2015

Chairman Johnson, Ranking Member Carper and distinguished members of the committee, I would like to thank you for the opportunity to share our members' perspectives on the recent announcements of agency data breaches impacting federal employees. I applaud you for holding this hearing on an extremely urgent issue for the federal workforce. As President of the National Treasury Employees Union (NTEU), I have the honor of representing over 150,000 federal workers in 31 agencies.

Mr. Chairman, as you can imagine, there is great fear and outrage on the part of federal employees and retirees in the wake of the U.S. Office of Personnel Management's (OPM) announcements on June 4th, and more recently on June 12th, that millions of current and former federal employees may have had significant personally identifiable information (PII) compromised owing to breaches in databases containing various personnel records. Federal employees have had a difficult few years, facing multi-year pay freezes, furloughs, sequestration, and this type of exposure of personal information is the final straw. Such exposure is simply unacceptable.

At the moment, a principal outstanding concern for federal employees and retirees is the confusion about what exact type of individual data and information was in fact compromised, and of whom. In its first statements, OPM confirmed that a breach had potentially compromised names, dates and places of birth, Social Security numbers, and addresses. However, a multitude of media and other public statements followed maintaining that the exposure was far greater in number and the information even more intrusive—that the type of information that may have been accessed by outsiders involved information about family members, beneficiary information from employee benefit programs, bank accounts, data submitted and stored from Declarations of Federal Employment and Standard Forms 85 and 86[i] (among others) as part of routine background investigations, including detailed financial information and medical history, home addresses and other PII and data for annuitants. Late on June 12th, OPM informed NTEU that this was indeed the case—that the worst case scenario for individuals' privacy—be they federal civilians, military personnel, contractors or other individuals simply appearing in various documents, and our nation's national security has occurred. However, NTEU wants to be clear that which employees have been affected by this apparent wider, and more serious breach, is still unknown to us and most importantly to the affected individuals.

OPM's statements issued to us and to agency heads still do not contain any information about who and what was affected in the second reported breach. We are not clear whether it affects individuals who possess security clearances, but perhaps also those who provide detailed information for suitability determinations and Standard Form 85 for public trust and critical non-sensitive positions. Not knowing whose data, and what exactly has been accessed and compromised, is creating widespread confusion and anxiety, on top of the general frustration of having one's personal information compromised be it from a foreign power, a thief, or otherwise ill-intended individual. Employees deserve to know what exact databases and information was hacked, and they need to be in a position to act, given the high level of risk they and their families are facing. It will also be important to address whether spouses, siblings, and other relatives, as well as former non-federal coworkers and acquaintances whose PII and contact information is provided, also had their information compromised, and whether there are plans to notify these members of the public, and to provide them with credit and identity protection services. We do not currently have any notification details to share with our members concerning the latest news from OPM, which again is unacceptable. I ask this Committee to ensure that the notification plan for all of these affected individuals is made public, and that it is put into action immediately.

Given that more than almost two weeks have passed since this wider breach was announced, NTEU believes it is time to immediately extend blanket credit monitoring and identity theft protection services to the entire federal workforce. We understand that the forensic investigation may take time, and that there are serious national security implications to this breach, so in order to best protect employees going forward, a blanket extension is needed. Since large numbers of employees (OPM estimates 2.1 million) have just received these services as part of the first OPM reported breach, it should be a relatively small number of additional employees who need this coverage extended to them.

OPM responded positively to NTEU's initial request that federal employees be allowed to use government computers in order to be able to contact CSID, the OPM-selected contractor, for credit monitoring purposes and to enroll in the identify theft protection services. Additionally, OPM also acted on NTEU's request to ensure access to government computers for those employees who do not regularly use computers on the job. While OPM has encouraged agencies to do these things, NTEU urges agency heads and this Committee to ensure that this access is indeed granted. An outstanding concern are many reports of employees not being able to access the CSID website owing to agency security systems that appear to be blocking this site.

It is critically important for employees and retirees to be able to access and enroll in protection services as soon as possible. We are being flooded with reports from our members demonstrating extensive problems when attempting to enroll in the CSID-provided services---ranging from not being able to reach an operator on the toll-free line, to significant call wait times, to the website crashing or freezing when individuals are attempting to enter the required enrollment information, to the rejection of assigned pin numbers and passwords, to the inability to establish required connectivity to the CSID website, to official email notifications going into spam filters, and to family members receiving the employee's notification letter, at an address that the employee has never lived at, or used for any purpose. We are also aware of notification letters addressed to the wrong individual or using a former name. In short, the CSID notification and enrollment process has been a disaster for many NTEU members. The damage caused by the breaches cannot be undone, but federal employees deserve a robust and functional response.

A major concern for employees is the delay in notification from the time of the actual discovery of the breaches. It is imperative that affected individuals receive swift notification of any type of breach compromising PII and other information. Any delay in notification only increases the likelihood of individuals experiencing identity theft and suffering financially. As you know, Mr. Chairman, NTEU represents employees at U.S. Customs and Border Protection (CBP), and in September 2014, the Department of Homeland Security (DHS) became aware of a breach involving KeyPoint, a contractor providing background investigations and support. The overall volume and sensitive type of information that is provided by employees undergoing a background investigation—either as a new hire or for a periodic reinvestigation—is significant, and includes extremely personal details of employees, their family members, and of their friends, and even of their coworkers and acquaintances. However, it was not until June 4, 2015 that DHS began providing and notifying CBP employees of their ability to enroll in credit monitoring and identity theft protection services. A nine month delay is simply unacceptable for all individuals involved. Moreover, two simultaneous, ongoing employee notification processes of compromised employee personnel records at CBP has led, not surprisingly, to major confusion in the workplace.

It is important to note that these breaches follow wide-scale breaches of health insurance carriers earlier this year that included federal employees enrolled in several Federal Employees Health Benefits Program (FEHBP) plans, and multiple announcements of agency breaches in 2014 affecting background investigation and suitability records. Federal employees are required to provide significant amounts of personal data to their employing agencies, for general employment purposes, as well as for suitability and security clearance purposes. NTEU asks that this Committee act to ensure that agencies have the ability to immediately safeguard federal employees' information going forward. It should come as no surprise that employees are questioning the idea of submitting this type of detailed personal information to their agencies in the future, and are particularly pointing to the suitability and security clearance process, forms, and storage as areas that need to be immediately changed.

Mr. Chairman, I also want to share that I have requested that, as we move forward, serious consideration be given by the Administration to providing both the credit monitoring services and the identity theft protection services for a significantly extended period of time beyond the current eighteen months. Given how long these breaches may have gone undetected, and since the exact identities and data compromised is not yet known, NTEU believes these items to be prudent courses of action. As an example, following this year's Blue Cross Blue Shield health care breaches, carriers provided twenty-four months of protective services to affected enrollees. Further, I want to re-iterate my call for immediate blanket coverage to be provided to those individuals affected in the second, apparent, more serious breach. Serious compromises of data and personal information demand serious responses from the U.S. government for the protection of its most valuable asset, its people. We also ask the Committee to keep these breaches in mind as serious consideration of so-called "Continuous Evaluation" (CE) policies move forward in the security clearance and suitability reform areas, as well as for oversight purposes of the Administration's Insider Threat program.

I again thank the Committee for the opportunity to provide NTEU's views on these alarming employee data breaches, and for your work to identify the source of these intrusions, as well as to identify the compromised employee records and personal information. And, most importantly to help ensure that this does not happen again. However, for the information already compromised, time is of the essence, and clear guidance and immediate notification, with adequate levels of protection, is warranted. Ultimately, NTEU members want to be assured that their information, and their family members' information, is not at risk because of their profession. Our members deserve to be able to trust that the government can properly secure their private information.

---

[1] Questionnaires for Public Trust, Non-Sensitive, and National Security Positions.

**Post-Hearing Questions for the Record
Submitted to the Honorable Katherine Archuleta
From Senator Rob Portman**

**"Under Attack: Federal Cybersecurity and the OPM Data Breach"
June 25, 2015**

1. Do you agree that the recent breaches of Office of Personnel Management (OPM) data make it all the more clear of the necessity to assess the current state of the federal government's cyber workforce and improve the federal government's ability to attract and recruit cybersecurity professionals?

   OPM: The Administration is already making progress in assessing the current state of the Federal cyber workforce and ways to improve the recruitment and retention of qualified cybersecurity professionals, but recognizes the growing need for additional talent going forward.

   OPM has the leadership role for the Administration's Initiative to Close Cybersecurity Skill Gaps.

   o This collaborative government-wide initiative involves partnering with the Office of Management and Budget and the Office of Science and Technology in the Executive Office of the President as well as interagency councils and the Federal agencies.
   o Currently we are mapping the existing Federal cybersecurity workforce using OPM's new Cybersecurity Data Element Standard that recognizes the value of the National Initiative for Cybersecurity Education (NICE) Framework.
   o Our goal is that this new dataset in FY2015 and beyond will be a driving force that aids Federal agencies in getting the workforce they need.
   o The re-categorizing of federal positions with cybersecurity work will tell us what skills are in demand and what skills need to be refreshed or developed.
   o Our job announcements will be designed to get the candidate quality desired by our hiring managers.
   o Our training and development opportunities will be better designed to sustain and get the workforce we need.

   In June 2003, OPM established a Government-wide Direct Hiring Authority to help in addressing the need for Information Technology professionals that specialize in information security which has helped to address many of the cyber security hiring needs across government. OPM has also issue agency-specific authority to Departments of Homeland Security and Defense to address their specific cyber missions.
   With regard to pay, agencies have considerable discretionary authority to provide additional compensation and leave benefits to support their recruitment and retention

efforts for cybersecurity employees. Information on pay and leave flexibilities is found here: http://www.opm.gov/policy-data-oversight/pay-leave/pay-and-leave-flexibilities-for-recruitment-and-retention/.

Encouraged Development of the workforce –NICE has focused on education, training, and workforce development to support the workforce required to meet our growing cybersecurity needs. NICE has worked with government and private sector organizations to develop the National Cybersecurity Workforce Framework to provide a standard lexicon for careers in this space, making it simpler for cybersecurity professionals to join the Federal workforce.

- In 2011, OPM issued a competency model for cybersecurity, found at: https://chcoc.usalearning.net/content/competency-model-cybersecurity. The model lists technical and general competencies by grade and by occupation (Information Technology, Electronics Engineering, Computer Engineering, and Telecommunications).

- OMB is leading a **Federal cyber workforce effort** to define the current gaps of cybersecurity talent throughout the government and outline current Hiring Authorities that can be used to bring in additional cybersecurity professionals; develop guidance related to these authorities; and promulgate tools and best practices to improve cybersecurity hiring.

- On May 29, 2015, the President signed the HERO Act into law. This Act provides veterans access to DHS' **online cybersecurity workforce training program** and an opportunity to continue serving the nation in the Immigration and Customs Enforcement Homeland Security Investigation's fight against cybercrime. DHS has also expanded access to this training program for employees of state, local, tribal, and territorial governments.

- OPM's objective, given the current fiscal environment, is to raise and leverage awareness of the Federal cybersecurity workforce across government. This includes ensuring that the public knows these positions are available and how to apply for them.

    o This awareness is being done primarily by working with technology departments at colleges and universities and promoting opportunities to compete for positions through the variety of mechanisms agencies use to fill these positions, including normal competitive hiring, the Pathways Programs, and other authorities. There are a variety of hiring flexibilities available to help to recruit and onboard STEM graduates.
    o Among these authorities is the Presidential Management Fellowship (PMF) program and the new PMF-STEM track, which has attracted applicants with

cybersecurity skills in disciplines such as computer science, computer engineering and computational analytics.
   o Our outreach guidance provides Federal agencies with up-to date information on how to message their opportunities, encourages them to work within their communities to strengthen the local talent pipeline in their communities, and provides workforce planning tools that enable them to plan for and get the workforce they need.

2. Is it true that 21.5 million people have been comprised by the Federal Investigative Services (FIS) data breach?

   OPM: OPM and the interagency incident response team have concluded with high confidence that sensitive information, including the Social Security Numbers (SSNs) of 21.5 million individuals was stolen from the background investigation databases. This includes 19.7 million individuals who applied for a background investigation, and 1.8 million non-applicants, primarily spouses or co-habitants of applicants.

3. What specific FIS computer system was compromised? Was the Personnel Investigations Processing System (PIPS) compromised?

   OPM: Information that is contained in PIPS was included in the data compromised in the breach.

4. What are the potential implications for the U.S. intelligence community resulting from the compromise of data on individuals who held or currently hold active security clearances, particularly in the case of information taken from the SF-86? Have you spoken to the Director of the FBI, the Director of National Intelligence, and the Secretary of Defense to discuss the potential implications to their operations?

   OPM: Questions about potential implications for the Intelligence Community (IC) are best answered by the IC. OPM has met with the ODNI and IC leadership and addressed their question to facilitate their ability to perform such an assessment. OPM has also remained in contact with the IC – including the FBI, ODNI and DoD – throughout the incident investigation and response, and has continued to coordinate closely with the IC throughout planning for notifications to affected individuals.

5. How are you working with other agencies to notify them of the impacts on their employees and in particular counter intelligence considerations?

OPM: OPM is working closely with its interagency partners, including the Department of Defense and the Office of the Director of National Intelligence, in response to the recent cyber security incidents. OPM is also in regular contact with agency leadership to update them on the process, including having each agency designate a Senior Accountable Official to coordinate communications and be a point of coordination as needed.

6. Can you confirm that $21 million is the total cost to be incurred by the federal government for credit monitoring and other safeguards provided to those affected by the incident involving personnel data?

   OPM: The initial cost of the contract to Winvale to provide credit monitoring and identity theft protection for 18 months to the 4.2 individuals affected by the personnel data breach is $21 million. The contract is structured such that OPM could incur additional costs based on the consumption of metered services (such as minutes at the call center) so the overall contract cost may increase modestly over time.

7. I understand that this is a fixed contract and is not dependent upon the number of individuals that sign up for the service. Is it true that OPM will not pay more than the approximate $21 million total for this service? Is there a cap on the number of individuals this contract will cover?

   OPM: The initial cost of the contract to Winvale to provide credit monitoring and identity theft protection for 18 months to the 4.2 individuals affected by the personnel data breach is $21 million. The contract is structured such that OPM could incur additional costs based on the consumption of metered services (such as minutes at the call center) so the overall contract cost may increase modestly over time.

8. Is it true that you are paying for this contract out of the Revolving Fund? If so, is your plan to recoup this money in the revolving fund by including it into the costs agencies pay for OPM services?

   OPM: OPM (EHRI) and DOI equally shared the cost of the contract. Since EHRI is part of the Revolving Fund, OPM will recover the OPM share of the cost of these services over a reasonable period through appropriate fees it charges agencies for EHRI.

9. According to the Defense Department's Cost Assessment and Program Evaluation office, the Defense Department incurs 75% of the background investigation costs that are paid to the revolving fund. Will the Defense Department be paying for 75%, or $15.7 million, for this contract? If so, are they aware of that? Are the other agencies paying into the Revolving Fund aware of this?

   OPM: As noted above, the cost of the breach relating to the incident involving personnel data will be borne equally, in the first instance, by OPM (EHRI) and DOI. OPM will recover its share of the costs over a reasonable period through the fees it charges agencies for EHRI. DoD's share of such fees will be calculated pursuant to the formula used for the EHRI activity, and not the percentage of background investigation costs attributable to DoD.

10. According to your testimony, the service offered by CSID to those whose personnel data was compromised is a comprehensive 18-month membership that includes credit report access, credit monitoring, identity theft insurance, and recovery services. Why is the comprehensive membership for those affected by the personnel breach limited to 18-months? Is it possible that the personally identifiable information comprised in the data breach, including social security numbers, could be used adversely by those responsible for the breach after the 18-month membership expires?

OPM: A careful and thoughtful analysis of the potential consequences of the personnel records incident as well as a review of the services available, precedent, and industry best practices led OPM and agency partners to conclude that 18 months was the appropriate duration for the comprehensive suite of services offered to help federal employees. The team continues to assess the appropriate duration of coverage, and will make adjustments as needed based on that ongoing assessment.

11. According to the OPM website, individuals affected by the background investigation incident will be provided with a suite of comprehensive services at no cost for at least three years, including full service identity restoration support and victim recovery assistance, identify theft insurance, identify monitoring for minor children, continuous credit monitoring, and fraud monitoring services beyond credit files. Why is the suite of comprehensive services for those affected by the background investigation incident being offered for at least three years? Will this service be extended to beyond three years? Why is the service offered to those affected by the background investigation incident being offered for at least twice as long as the service provided to those affected by the incident involving personnel data?

OPM: The protections in the suite of services to be offered to individuals who were affected by the background investigation incident are tailored to address the circumstances of this particular incident, and will be provided for a period of at least three years. Based on the team's ongoing assessments over time, the Government may provide additional coverage associated with the background investigation incident, as needed. Limiting the first task order to three years will allow the Government to adapt and provide the most up-to-date services. The three-year service length also will allow future policy to reflect new information developed by the interagency group that is being convened to develop, in consultation with stakeholders, a longer-term proposal for Federal employee identity protection.

12. Will the service for those affected by the background investigation incident require an additional contract or amend the original contract for those affected by the incident involving personnel data? Will this increase the cost of providing services beyond what was agreed to in the contract for those affected by the incident involving personnel data?

OPM: [As of June 25, 2015] OPM is currently partnering with the Department of Defense to identify a private-sector firm that specializes in credit and identity theft monitoring in order to provide a comprehensive suite of services designed to help individuals minimize potential risks from this incident. Based on the team's ongoing assessments over time, the Government may provide additional coverage associated with this incident, as needed. Limiting the first task order to three years will allow the Government to adapt and provide the most up-to-date services. The three-year service length also will allow future policy to reflect new information developed by the interagency group that is being convened to develop, in consultation with stakeholders, a longer-term proposal for Federal employee identity protection.

[As of September 10, 2015] On September 1, 2015, OPM and the Department of Defense announced the award of a contract for approximately $133 million to Identity Theft Guard Solutions LLC, doing business as ID Experts, for identity theft protection services for 21.5 million individuals whose personal information was stolen in the incident involving background investigations.

Post-Hearing Questions for the Record
Submitted to Hon. Katherine Archuleta
From Senator Claire McCaskill

"Under Attack: Federal Cybersecurity and the OPM Data Breach"

June 25, 2015

After a data breach in March 2014, the Office of Personnel Management (OPM) developed a plan to make major security improvements to the existing IT environment. But sometime during that process, according to the OPM Office of the Inspector General (IG), OPM determined that it would be more effective to completely overhaul the agency's IT infrastructure.

1. How did OPM define "effective?"

   OPM: Working with the Department of Homeland Security and its interagency partners – including the Department of Defense – during the incident response, OPM recognized that the current network architecture presented limitations in achieving an optimized level of security. We evaluated recommendations from the OPM Inspector General (IG) and the Government Accountability Office and considered best practices in cyber security. As a result, OPM identified a need to redesign the architecture of its infrastructure to achieve a more secure posture. OPM will continue to consult with the IG and keep both the IG and Congress informed about progress throughout this project.

2. Was a cost comparison done between updating the old infrastructure and completely overhauling it or was this based entirely on maximizing security?

   OPM: Using the old infrastructure was not an option. The risk of latent malicious software on old systems would not have achieved OPM's security goals, and the network in place at the time did not lend itself to modernization. In addition, much of OPM's hardware was near, or at, end-of-life, meaning OPM needed to procure new hardware anyway. Accordingly, it also would not have been cost-effective to update old infrastructure.

According to the flash audit, OPM is still in the process of evaluating its existing IT architecture, and had failed to complete several critical preliminary steps before awarding the contract. Specifically, the IG found that OPM had not yet identified the full scope and cost of this IT infrastructure project; had not prepared a Major IT Business Case for this project; does not have a comprehensive list of stakeholders; had not conducted a feasibility study; does not have a budgetary justification; has not completed an impact assessment for existing systems and stakeholders; has not completed a quality assurance plan and procedures for contractor oversight; has not completed a technological infrastructure acquisition plan; has not completed a high level test and evaluation plan; and has not completed an implementation plan.

3. Have any of these steps been taken since the date of the audit?

OPM: The Office of the Chief Information Officer will update project documentation and submit a current business plan in September. OPM is committed to justifying program funding and tracking how funds are spent. We are linking our expenditures to the plan provided by the interagency response team in order to justify expenditures and link them to recommended security capabilities. OPM is working closely with OMB and our stakeholders to enhance the transparency, documentation, tracking, and justification for this information technology project.

OPM has indicated that the entire project will cost $93 million and take 18-24 months.

4. What are these estimate based on, what entity produced these estimates, and has anyone outside of OPM or the contractor bidding on the project, verified these estimates?

OPM: OPM based its implementation plan and cost estimates on a remediation plan coordinated with OMB and OPM's interagency partners – including the Department of Homeland Security, and the Department of Defense -- and in consultation with cyber experts in both the public and private sectors. OPM is tracking its expenditures to this plan and the project is currently operating within reasonable estimates.

5. Is this project on the IT Dashboard? If not, why not?

OPM: This project does not appear on the IT Dashboard because, due to the unique and compelling circumstances, it was initiated outside of the typical major business case submission cycle. OPM expects that once project documentation is updated and a current business plan is submitted, the project will be added to the IT Dashboard.

As OPM is now aware, the Special Inspector General for Afghanistan Reconstruction (SIGAR) raised concerns about $135 million in unsubstantiated costs by the contractor for projects in Afghanistan, and employees of the contractor were found to have engaged in inappropriate behavior. You made reference during a House Oversight and Government Reform hearing on June 24, 2015 that the contracting officers had a process for vetting the contractor, which used to be called Jorge Scientific and now goes by the name Imperatis

6. What specific steps were taken to vet the contractor? Did OPM talk to SIGAR about its findings?

OPM: OPM sought contract services to support critical efforts to enhance the security of IT systems and its network through an interagency agreement with the Department of Homeland Security. Imperatis was identified as having the relevant experience and depth of expertise necessary to meet OPM's urgent need. OPM and DHS monitor contractor performance on an ongoing basis and will continue to do so as these important IT modernization initiatives progress. We would refer any further questions on this topic to the Department of Homeland Security contracting office.

I understand that the justification for the sole-source contract was the urgency of improving the security of OPM's current IT systems. However, according to the IG, the sole-source contract extends to all four phases of OPM's planned IT overhaul and will take at least two years. In addition, it is my understanding that four phases of this project require different expertise.

7. What was the justification for awarding the sole source contract for all four phases of the IT transition?

   OPM: In response to the urgent need to secure the existing environment, OPM awarded a sole source contract to Imperatis, consistent with Federal contracting and procurement requirements and Office of Management and Budget guidance. Based on past performance, OPM identified Imperatis as a company with the relevant experience necessary to meet the full network and security engineering support needed for this requirement. The contract is primarily for the first two of the four phases of the infrastructure improvement project, or the Tactical and Shell phases. Although the contract contemplates that Imperatis will have work to do in all four phases, not all aspects of the work required by OPM in phases three and four are included in the contract with Imperatis. For phases three and four – Migration and Cleanup – Imperatis's role under the contract will consist of preparation and support, a role necessitated by the expertise and knowledge they have developed during the design and implementation of the Shell (phase two), and will not include other components of phases three and four such as systems modernization (phase three) and disposal of decommissioned equipment (phase four). OPM will determine the appropriate acquisition strategy or strategies to accomplish the modernization of business applications, as needed. With respect to the disposal of decommissioned equipment, OPM does not intend that Imperatis will dispose of decommissioned equipment; that element of the Cleanup will be done through the existing OPM process.

8. During the past 30 years, administrations have spent more than $100 million trying to automate OPM's management of federal retirement paperwork. In 1987 OPM spent about $25 million on an automation project. 10 years later, OPM pulled the plug on the project, and in 1997, it started over.

   First it tried revamping the system in-house. Then it scrapped that plan and hired contractors. After years of work, the system the contractors built was supposed to be ready by early 2008. Stop me if this sounds familiar. The system went live in 2008 after $105 million was sunk into it, and it was a spectacular failure.

   What lessons were learned from those experiences and applied to the current IT overhaul effort?

   OPM: We developed a Strategic IT Plan to help ensure our IT supports and aligns to OPM's Strategic Plan, and that the Agency's mission is fulfilled. We have adopted six successful practices– IT Leadership, IT Governance, Enterprise Architecture, Agile IT, Data Analytics and Information Security. Additionally, the Plan identifies enterprise and business initiatives that are moving the Agency's IT forward. We are using an incremental approach in bringing existing and future capabilities onto a shared platform for more rational and efficient data exchange and work processes. We are measuring the performance of our IT program using three basic metrics: compliance with laws, policies, and successful practices; user and stakeholder satisfaction with improved IT capabilities; and cost per IT service or transaction. The OPM Strategic IT Plan establishes leadership, a governance structure and an agile environment that will help guard against IT development failures. Each individual IT project is managed to a project plan, with detailed accountability metrics, by a certified program manager. We are building a more robust enterprise architecture to tear down silos within the agency, eliminate duplication and identify enterprise opportunities, rather than program office-specific IT solutions. This approach allows us to make the most of our limited resources and fosters a culture of collaboration.

Post-Hearing Questions for the Record
Submitted to the Honorable Katherine Archuleta
From Senator Heidi Heitkamp

"Under Attack: Cybersecurity & the OPM Data Breach"
June 25, 2015

1. Congress, as an entity, understands the importance of cooperation between the Executive and the Legislative branches in resolving the issues that affect the American people. Subsequently, how can Congress assist OPM in dealing with the breach and preventing another breach of this magnitude?

   OPM: Several Members have asked where additional funding could help accelerate the process of improving our data security protections going forward. While OPM has secured its current legacy environment as best possible, a significant cyber security risk remains every day that OPM continues to operate in this legacy environment. Through prioritization of existing resources in FY 2014 and FY 2015, OPM designed and built a new, modern and secure infrastructure environment that will provide improved protections to business applications and high value data assets. The $37 million, in addition to the President's FY 2016 Budget request for $21 million, would allow OPM to accelerate its efforts to expedite the modernization and migration of retirement services and background investigation systems to the more secure IT environment and provide additional staff, both federal and contractors, to support this migration effort. Without the funds in FY 2016, OPM's applications will remain outside of the secure infrastructures, until such time as funds are made available—at this point in time, that is likely FY 2017. To further explain, these additional resources would allow OPM to immediately begin the necessary steps to migrate retirement services and background investigation applications rather than waiting for pricing increases to pay for the migration of these services in the next budget cycle, which is the "traditional" way these programs have operated. The Administration has also proposed legislation to share information so that they can enhance their security protections in near real time, reducing phishing attacks and the spread of malicious software.

2. What actions are OPM considering taking for decreasing the value of the information that the intruders may have obtained? For example, is OPM considering facilitating the issuance of new social security numbers to individuals affected by the data breach?

   OPM: OPM is working with its interagency partners, including the Social Security Administration, the Internal Revenue Service, and the Department of State to protect against fraud or potential misuse of the information that may have been stolen in the recent cyber security incidents. Additionally, OPM is encouraging all potentially affected individuals to use best practices to protect their information online and available resources, such as the Federal Trade Commission's identifytheft.gov website and OPM's website, opm.gov/cybersecurity/.

3. Given the severity of the data breach, many federal employees, understandably, have a heightened apprehension towards sharing personally identifiable information. Why is it beneficial for OPM to use a third-party contractor to send notices to affected employees as opposed to OPM sending formal notices?

OPM: To quickly notify individuals impacted by the personnel records incident, OPM selected a third party vendor that had expertise and resources to provide the necessary services. OPM is working with the Department of Defense and the General Services Administration to provide notifications and contract services to those impacted by the background investigations incident. The Department of Defense will issue the notifications to the affected individuals.

4. Has OPM consulted the Department of Defense concerning their current strategy for thwarting cyberattacks? If not, please explain.

   a. How can OPM learn from effective cybersecurity strategies employed by the Department of Defense or any other relevant federal agency?

OPM: OPM has worked with the Department of Homeland Security and its interagency partners – including the Department of Defense (DOD) – since the discovery of the data incident. DOD has provided incident response services, host platform assessments, and web application stress testing. OPM has also been provided with mitigation recommendations from the interagency response team. As OPM analyzes and implements these recommendations, it will continue to work with DHS and its interagency partners – including the Department of Defense.

Post-Hearing Questions for the Record
Submitted to Mr. Tony Scott
From Senator Rob Portman

"Under Attack: Federal Cybersecurity and the OPM Data Breach"
June 25, 2015

1. **Do you agree that the recent Office of Personnel Management (OPM) data breaches make it all the more clear of the necessity to assess the current state of the federal government's cyber workforce and improve the federal government's ability to attract and recruit cybersecurity professionals?**

   To ensure that Federal agencies are dedicating appropriate attention and resources to address these critical and pressing challenges, OMB initiated a Cybersecurity Sprint on June 12, 2015. The Cybersecurity Sprint required agencies to take immediate steps to further protect Federal information and assets and improve the resilience of Federal networks. These actions included implementing strong user identity verification and authentication, patching critical vulnerabilities, scanning for cyber threat indicators, identifying critical information assets, and reviewing and reducing the number of privileged user accounts. In addition to providing direction to agencies, we established a Sprint Team to lead a 30-day review of the Federal Government's cybersecurity policies, procedures, and practices. Accordingly, we tasked the Sprint Team with creating and operationalizing a set of action plans and strategies to further address critical cybersecurity priorities and recommend a Federal civilian cybersecurity strategy. The result of those recommendations is the Cybersecurity Strategy and Implementation Plan (CSIP). The action items outlined in the CSIP will strengthen the government's cybersecurity protections and reduce the risk to our Federal IT ecosystem. One of the main areas of focus in the CSIP deals with the Federal government's ability to recruit and retain a highly-qualify cybersecurity workforce. The CSIP identifies concrete steps Federal agencies can take to address this gap in cybersecurity talent.

2. **Is it true that 21.5 million people have been comprised by the Federal Investigative Services (FIS) data breach?**

   OPM has concluded with high confidence that sensitive information, including the Social Security Numbers (SSNs) of 21.5 million individuals, was stolen from the background investigation databases. I will defer to OPM for specific details concerning the breach.

3. **What specific FIS computer system was compromised? Was the Personnel Investigations Processing System (PIPS) compromised?**

   I will defer to OPM regarding which systems were compromised.

Post-Hearing Questions for the Record
Submitted to Andy Ozment, Ph.D.
From Senator Heidi Heitkamp

"Under Attack: Federal Cybersecurity and the OPM Data Breach"
June 25, 2015

Question: In your testimony you said that the breach is not a uniquely governmental issue. What strategies or tools are private companies, who have been previously breached, using to prevent data breaches?

Furthermore, how is the Department of Homeland Security collaborating with private companies who are developing significant protective measures?

Response: As a first principle, security cannot be achieved through only one type of tool. That is why security professionals believe in defense-in-depth: employing multiple tools in combination to manage the risks of cyber attacks. There is no "silver bullet" to defeat cyber threats. DHS works with private companies to focus on three areas: encouraging adoption of best practices, sharing actionable cybersecurity information quickly and widely, and effectively responding to incidents when they occur.

Many cybersecurity threats can be stopped by implementing best practices.[1] These best practices can be expensive to implement—particularly when the organization is large or complex—but many are relatively low cost. However, investing the time and resources in implementing best practices provides organizations a baseline from which to manage cybersecurity risk. By disseminating and promoting cybersecurity best practices, particularly those captured in the Cybersecurity Framework, DHS helps private sector stakeholders build their own capacity to more quickly detect and block threats, mitigate vulnerabilities, and respond to incidents. DHS offers risk assessment methods to help companies understand their cybersecurity posture and identify key areas of improvement through the Critical Infrastructure Cybersecurity Voluntary Program (known as C-Cubed VP). DHS can assist private sector partners with on-site technical assistance to support partner use of these methods and tools by providing the materials for partner to use on its own. Further, DHS works with boards of directors and company officers to facilitate executive-level recognition of cybersecurity best practices' value, and impress upon them the need to institutionalize them throughout their organization.

Information sharing is a particular focal area for DHS in our cybersecurity efforts, as the Department's missions intersect with the private sector, law enforcement, intelligence,

---

[1] An example of a simple best practice is to require complicated passwords when logging into computers. An example of a more complicated best practice is to segment your network and carefully monitor it for intrusions.

Question#:	1
Topic:	data breaches
Hearing:	Under Attack: Federal Cybersecurity and the OPM Data Breach
Primary:	The Honorable Heidi Heitkamp
Committee:	HOMELAND SECURITY (SENATE)

and efforts to protect the government's networks, systems and data. Because of our unique vantage point, the information we receive from our partners allows us to provide critical situational awareness with other partners—with due consideration for protecting privacy, liberties and confidentiality. In particular, when we detect an attempted attack or intrusion against the government, we learn from it and use it to better protect ourselves and our partners. Information sharing must be tailored to the particular requirements of the recipient organization and reflective of the various types and uses of cybersecurity information. To this end, DHS engages in information sharing with government and private sector partners in five primary ways:

- In-person information sharing on the National Cybersecurity and Communications Integration Center (NCCIC) watch floor
- Bilateral sharing of cyber threat indicators, including via the Cyber Information Sharing and Collaboration Program and through automated sharing and receipt of cyber threat indicators
- As-needed information sharing via standing groups
- Broad dissemination of alerts and bulletins
- Strategic engagement and collaboration

Real-Time Collaboration on the NCCIC Watch Floor
The NCCIC, as codified by the National Cybersecurity Protection Act of 2014, serves as a central hub for cybersecurity information sharing between federal agencies, the private sector, law enforcement, and the intelligence community. Through a 24x7 watch floor, the NCCIC provides a forum for real-time collaboration to understand and gain situational awareness of cybersecurity incidents and risks. Currently, representatives from DHS law enforcement agencies (U.S Secret Service, Immigration and Customs Enforcement/Homeland Security Investigations), from several federal agencies (FBI, USNORTHCOM, USCYBERCOM, NSA. Department of Treasury, and Department of Energy) and four Information Sharing and Analysis Centers (ISACs; representing the financial, aviation, and energy sectors as well as state, local, tribal, and territorial governments) have dedicated liaisons on the NCCIC watch floor. Further, 114 private sector companies have as-needed access to the NCCIC through their participation in the Cyber Information Sharing and Collaboration Program (CISCP), discussed further below.

Bi-Directional Sharing of Cyber Threat Indicators
A key element of DHS's information sharing approach for public and private sector partners is to share cyber threat indicators widely and continue efforts to be able to

Question#:	1
Topic:	data breaches
Hearing:	Under Attack: Federal Cybersecurity and the OPM Data Breach
Primary:	The Honorable Heidi Heitkamp
Committee:	HOMELAND SECURITY (SENATE)

conduct this sharing at machine speed in formats that can be immediately used for network defense.[2] Our goal is thus to broaden the base and increase the speed of information sharing to help ensure that an adversary can only use a given attack one time before it is blocked by all other government and private sector partners – increasing the attacker's costs and reducing the prevalence of damaging cybersecurity incidents.

The Cyber Information Sharing and Collaboration Program (CISCP) enables information sharing and enhances collaboration with our private sector partners. CISCP provides a platform and a trusted forum for exchanging threat and vulnerability information, governed by a Cooperative Research and Development Agreement (CRADA) between DHS and each CISCP participant. The CRADA allows participants to gain as-needed access to the NCCIC, a mechanism to receive security clearances, and the ability to participate in bi-directional information sharing. Currently, information sharing in CISCP is conducted via secure e-mail or an online portal.

Moving forward, DHS is beginning to share "machine-readable" cyber threat indicators automatically and in near-real time automated indicator sharing. Automated indicator sharing uses the DHS-developed Structured Threat Information eXpression™/Trusted Automated eXchange of Indicator Information™ (STIX/TAXII) formats, a mechanism for sharing cyber threat information in a common manner. In brief, STIX/TAXII allows public and private sector partners to share cyber threat information in the same way so that computers can immediately use the information for network defense. Cybersecurity vendors are now integrating STIX/TAXII into their commercial products, further broadening use of the standard. DHS is already using this initiative to distribute (uni-directionally) machine-readable cyber threat indicators at near-real-time to one government agency. We are working now to expand recipients across the public and private sectors. Companies participating in CISCP are expected to be the first participants in automated information sharing, via an addendum to their current CISCP CRADA. DHS expects

---

[2] Examples of cyber threat indicators include malicious email addresses or Internet Protocol (IP addresses). DHS reviews all cyber threat indicators for privacy, civil liberties and other compliance concerns. Currently, these reviews are conducted by human analysis. With automated indicator sharing, we will continue to review all indicators, but will transition to rely substantially on a rules-based approach that combines automated and human review. This will ensure that all privacy, civil liberties, and other compliance concerns are proactively identified and mitigated while minimizing time delays and resource requirements currently associated with such analysis.

Question#:	1
Topic:	data breaches
Hearing:	Under Attack: Federal Cybersecurity and the OPM Data Breach
Primary:	The Honorable Heidi Heitkamp
Committee:	HOMELAND SECURITY (SENATE)

to begin bidirectional information sharing (dissemination and receipt) with private sector companies by December 2015.

Standing Information Sharing Groups
During a cybersecurity incident or in response to an exigent risk, it is essential to convene appropriate entities to quickly share information and promulgate necessary mitigations. With the private sector, the NCCIC shares emergent information via the Cyber Unified Coordination Group (UGC). The UCG consists of senior representatives from key federal agencies, major companies across critical infrastructure sectors, and state, local, tribal, and territorial governments. During a significant incident, the UCG is the principal mechanism to collaborate with key private sector partners in a secure forum and plan integrated responses that appropriately incorporate priorities from the government and private sector.

Cybersecurity Alerts, Bulletins, and Other Messages
The NCCIC develops and disseminates alerts and bulletins via e-mail, on public websites, and through secure online portals. These alerts and bulletins provide detailed technical guidance and context that security professionals use to both understand the particular risk and implement effective mitigations. In FY14, the NCCIC disseminated nearly 12,000 alerts, bulletins, and other products to approximately 100,000 recipients.

Strategic Engagement and Collaboration
DHS convenes partners to understand cybersecurity risks and share best practices. Through fora such as Advanced Threat Technical Exchanges that bring together cross-sector companies participating in CISCP, such collaboration also helps participating organizations gain context into the intricacies of specific cybersecurity risks. As the Sector-Specific Agency for the Information Technology and Communications sectors and the Federal Government's lead for critical infrastructure protection, DHS serves a key role as a convening organization between the public and private sectors.

Finally, DHS coordinates the federal response to significant incidents at the request of the victim company. Cybersecurity is about risk management because it is not feasible to eliminate all risk. Companies that implement best practices and share information will help increase the cost for adversaries while thwarting many threats. However, adversaries are persistent and quickly evolve tactics and techniques to achieve their goal. Companies must have the capability to quickly detect and respond to incidents, and DHS has a role to both assist them and to coordinate the national response to significant incidents. When companies experience a major incident, DHS offers on-site or remote incident response

Question#:	1
Topic:	data breaches
Hearing:	Under Attack: Federal Cybersecurity and the OPM Data Breach
Primary:	The Honorable Heidi Heitkamp
Committee:	HOMELAND SECURITY (SENATE)

assistance that helps protect affected companies directly by identifying the extent of the compromise, expelling the intruder from the victim network, offering technical mitigations to help the victim restore their networks to a more secure state, and when appropriate, undertaking a law enforcement investigation to pursue to malicious actor.

Question: Furthermore, how is the Department of Homeland Security collaborating with private companies who are developing significant protective measures?

Response: DHS works closely with the private sector to understand, inform, and pilot emerging cybersecurity innovations. An example of this collaboration is STIX/TAXII, which enables public and private sector partners to share cyber threat information in a standardized manner so that the information can be used in near-real time for network defense. DHS believes that the promulgation of a consistent information sharing "language" will accelerate and simplify collaboration in this space, thereby increasing the volume of shared cyber threat information and correspondingly its protective value. Recognizing this opportunity, DHS closely collaborated with a wide range of private companies, academics, and international partners to develop STIX/TAXII, gain wide industry acceptance, and recently submitted STIX/TAXII to an international standards body for formal adoption as an international standard. STIX/TAXII is now being implemented in security products across industry, and forms the basis for numerous information sharing tools, including those produced by partners such as the Financial Services-Information Sharing and Analysis Center.

DHS also relies on innovation in the private sector to ensure that our programs protecting the Federal Government are effective against emerging cybersecurity threats. As we fully deploy the EINSTEIN 3A intrusion prevention system, we are mindful that to stay ahead of the adversary, we must go beyond the current approach that uses indicators of known threats. We are examining best-in-class technologies from the private sector to evolve to this next stage of network defense. Further, we are piloting advanced malware detection and anomaly analysis capabilities based upon leading commercial tools that are designed to automatically identify and separate suspicious traffic for further inspection, even if the precise indicator has not been seen before. Finally, the Continuous Diagnostics and Mitigation (CDM) program, which provides federal civilian executive branch agencies with tools to identify and prioritize risks on their own networks, is based entirely on commercial tools. As DHS plans for Phases 2 and 3 of this program, which focus on identifying malicious users and events on federal networks, respectively, we are closely engaged with private companies to identify and test products that could bring innovative security benefits to this program.

Question#:	1
Topic:	data breaches
Hearing:	Under Attack: Federal Cybersecurity and the OPM Data Breach
Primary:	The Honorable Heidi Heitkamp
Committee:	HOMELAND SECURITY (SENATE)

DHS NPPD also leverages research and development funded by the Science and Technology Directorate's, Cyber Security Division (CSD), much of which is with private sector research firms, or technologies that are transitioning into commercial use. For example, DHS CSD funded a pilot deployment of Hyperion, a malware forensics and software assurance technology with US-CERT. Hyperion was originally developed by Oak Ridge National Laboratory, but was licensed to a private company R&K Cyber Solutions, LLC in February 2015.

Post-Hearing Questions for the Record
Submitted to Andy Ozment, Ph.D.
From Senator Rob Portman

"Under Attack: Federal Cybersecurity and the OPM Data Breach"
June 25, 2015

Question: Do you agree that the recent Office of Personnel Management (OPM) data breaches make it all the more clear of the necessity to assess the current state of the federal government's cyber workforce and improve the federal government's ability to attract and recruit cybersecurity professionals?

Response: Yes. Federal agencies and the private sector face persistent and sophisticated adversaries and will continue to experience frequent attempted intrusions. An adequately sized and well-qualified workforce is necessary to manage this risk. DHS thanks Congress for providing much-needed flexibility and authorities in the Border Patrol Pay Reform Act of 2014. Implementation of this critical legislation will greatly help DHS recruit, hire, and retain the best-in-class workforce needed for our essential cybersecurity mission.